Jan. 16, 1997

Ted —
Thanks for the love and support.

Love,
Ken

A New Lease on Life

Jan. 16, 1997

Ted — Thank you for everything. You can write your book about your adventures with us. Love,
Madge

A New
Lease
on Life

Facing the World after a Suicide Attempt

John A Chabot, Ph.D.

Fairview Press
Minneapolis

Published by Fairview Press, 2450 Riverside Avenue South, Minneapolis, MN 55454.

Library of Congress Cataloging-in-Publication Data
Chabot, John A., 1945–
A new lease on life : facing the world after a suicide attempt /
John A. Chabot
     p.   cm.
Includes bibliographical references.
ISBN 1-57749-009-6
     1. Suicidal behavior.   I. Title
RC569.C47   1997
362.2'8—dc20   96-35265
                                                          CIP

First Printing: January 1997

Printed in the United States of America
01 00 99 98 97   7 6 5 4 3 2 1

Cover design: Circus Design
Author photo: Michael M. Fairchild, Photo Synthesis, Inc.

The author gratefully acknowledges the permission of Mary W. Mannhardt to use excerpts from her book *Dark Marathon: The Mary Wazeter Story* (Zondervan, 1989).

Publisher's Note: Fairview Press publishes books and other materials related to the subjects of social and family issues. Its publications, including *A New Lease on Life*, do not necessarily reflect the philosophy of Fairview Hospital and Healthcare Services or their treatment programs.

For a free catalog of Fairview Press titles, call toll-free 1-800-544-8207.

*To my wife, Marcia, and my daughters, Kim and Amy,
for their patient understanding, their creative
encouragement, and their loving acceptance.*

I will not raise my hand against myself on account of pain, for so to die is to be conquered. But I know that if I must suffer without hope of relief, I will depart, not through fear of the pain itself, but because it prevents all for which I would live.

—Lucius Annaeus Seneca

Contents

Acknowledgments

A project such as this represents a labor of love attributable to many special people. First and foremost, I owe many thanks to the eight courageous individuals whose exposed lives constitute the core of this book. Their candid openness during the interviews and their thoughtful revisions of the manuscript helped me to shoulder the awesome responsibility of relating their stories as accurately and completely as possible.

Special gratitude is due Dr. David Conroy who generously shared his own work in suicide education. He was instrumental in connecting me with several of those who ultimately agreed to be interviewed for this project. Thanks go as well to Dr. Lisa Firestone and Dr. George Stricker for their supportive encouragement and their valuable help in making important introductions.

To my friend, Ulric Sorensen, go many thanks for the creative word-crafting suggestions during critical stages of the writing. My gratitude also extends to Lane Stiles, my editor at Fairview Press, who provided both valuable assistance and warm encouragement through to completion of the book. Finally, a special word of acknowledgment to my friend and colleague, Dr. Michael Gorkin, who was there for the genesis of this project. He has remained an inspiration to me through his own writing over the years.

To all these individuals, both named and anonymous, this book is the culmination of many heads, many hands, and many hearts working together to give something important back to the world. This work represents a renewal of our own respective leases on life as we contemplate why we are still here and what we hope to leave behind as we move on.

Preface

I first developed an interest in the psychological dynamics of death and dying nearly thirty years ago as a graduate student pursuing my doctorate in clinical psychology. As my journey of discovery unfolded over the years, I found myself considering a rather simple and straightforward thesis: that the way people face death is a direct reflection of the way they have lived their lives. Those individuals who experience life as meaningless, threatening, and painful will face death with corresponding anxiety, hopelessness, and dread. Those people who have led more autonomous lives filled with dignity and purpose will bring these same qualities to bear as they face inevitable death with resilience and perhaps even courage.

But what about those who choose to end their lives through suicide rather than allow destiny to determine their fateful end? What makes anyone seriously consider suicide as a solution to life crisis? Does the suicide attempt itself reflect the same resignation and fearfulness that the individual experienced in life, or is it an attempt to conquer the fear of death, to take away its sting? Is that final act an attempt to give ultimate meaning and purpose to the last moment of life, to sever once and forever the unbearable suffering and pain?

These fundamental questions have been pursued by philosophers and theologians for centuries. Science eventually entered the quest, and the search for answers has inspired research studies and academic exploration designed to unravel the enigma surrounding suicide. Public discussion of death and dying were considered taboo thirty years ago. Few articles and books were available in either professional or popular literature. Recent years have witnessed a proliferation of writing on death and dying, however, with many books reaching the best-seller lists, well within the mainstream of public consumption. The subject of suicide has taken longer to emerge from the shadows, and in fact remains a controversial topic of discussion. In this age of Derek Humphry's *Final Exit* and Dr. Kevorkian's obsessive campaign, the legal and moral debate about assisted suicide and the right to die with dignity rages on. Meanwhile, the literature on suicide continues to grow.

This is not just another book about suicide. The focal point of these eight stories, these eight lives in progress, is on living after the suicidal crisis, not the suicide attempt itself. Those factors that contributed to the suicide attempt are relegated to the backdrop. After failing to complete their final act of self-destruction and living to face the next day, these people are confronted with having to negotiate a new lease on life. This book explores their journeys of healing toward successful recovery.

For those who entertain suicidal ideas and impulses, it is important to envision how life goes on rather than detail the many ways people attempt to die. For professionals who work with such individuals, it is invaluable to learn how people move back from the edge and repair their lives. Beyond the difficult task of predicting a suicide attempt, understanding the process of recovery plays a critical role in preventing an escalating crisis. Moreover, focusing on successful recovery rather than the suicide attempt necessarily switches the focus from endless probing into self-destructive urges to exploring healthy ways of coping and practical methods for rebuilding one's life.

This recovery-based approach is most valuable to those contemplating suicide themselves, and to their family and friends who are struggling to provide emotional support. Through these stories of real people struggling with real crises and real resolutions, we are all compelled to confront our own perceptions about living life and facing death.

1

It's Not Always Such a Wonderful Life

After all this, I have to admit that I am a failed suicide. It is a dismal confession to make, since nothing, really, would seem to be easier than to take your own life. Seneca, the final authority on the subject, pointed out disdainfully that the exits are everywhere: each precipice and river, each branch of every tree, every vein in your body will set you free. . . . I built up to the act carefully and for a long time, with a kind of blank pertinacity. It was the one constant focus of my life, making everything else irrelevant, a diversion. . . . At no point was there any question . . . of changing the direction of the journey. Yet, despite all that, I never quite made it.

—A. Alvarez, *The Savage God: A Study of Suicide*

Understanding suicidal crisis in the lives of desperate people is knowing the story of enduring, insurmountable pain—pain which exceeds the ability to cope and overshadows the fear of death. Some would say that suicide is not a freely chosen, voluntary, or intentional act, but is rather the inevitable consequence of unrelieved pain and suffering. Others might conclude that suicide represents the ultimate control over life itself, a final attempt to assert an illusion of power in a world which continuously reminds of one's pervasive powerlessness. It is as if the failure to experience control in life can be compensated by a final act of mastery over the way to end that life, the way one faces deliberate death. To the suicidal individual, death becomes the final solution to the unbearable pain of living.

The romanticized version of people facing suicidal crisis and stepping back from the edge is reflected in the classic holiday favorite, *It's a Wonderful Life*. In the film, director Frank Capra captures the soul of despair as George Bailey, Jimmy Stewart's character, stands poised to jump from the bridge, wishing he had never been born. Clutching the smallest shred of hope, he is coaxed to safety by his guardian angel, Clarence, who guides Bailey through a review of his life, convincing him of his importance to others.

In a dramatic denouement on a snowy winter night, Bailey returns to the bridge, pleading for another chance at life. "I want to live!" Bailey cries into the frigid night air. "Please, God, let me live again!" In the tearful finale, Bailey finds himself exhilarated to be alive, basking in the rousing support of his family and friends. He is filled with gratitude for the angel who brought him back from the brink of suicidal desperation.

That is Hollywood's version of suicidal crisis, of course. In real life, angels can be hard to find when they are needed most. And for those who have to face the world after their failed suicide attempt, life is not always so wonderful. English poet and critic A. Alvarez noted the lingering despair in the

2

aftermath of his own failed suicide attempt:

> Above all, I was disappointed. Somehow, I felt, death had let me down; I had expected more of it. I had looked for something overwhelming, an experience which would clarify all my confusions . . . a synoptic vision of life, crisis by crisis, all suddenly explained, justified, redeemed, a Last Judgment in the coils and circuits of the brain. . . . But it turned out to be denial of experience. . . . I'd been swindled.

Each story that follows relates a different version of life after a failed suicide attempt. For a few, survival may have had miraculous dimensions, not unlike those provided by guardian angels. Indeed, it is difficult to understand how they managed to survive without considering the possibility of divine intervention.

For the majority, however, survival is burdened by emotional traumas and physical scars, further compounding the pain and despair that preceded the attempt. For one individual, her new lease on life means learning to live as a paraplegic with chronic pain, the lasting legacy of her fall from a bridge. Another is blind in one eye, a constant reminder of her failed suicide attempt. Yet another survived his suicidal crisis only to later be diagnosed HIV positive, and have to live with the ominous threat of dying from AIDs looming over his head.

Beyond feelings of relief and a sense of miraculous salvation, these survivors' stories chronicle the ongoing struggles with ambivalence and anxiety, guilt and despair that followed their suicide attempts. In the process of playing the hand they've been dealt, they reveal the human capacity to rebound, persevere, and triumph despite the obstacles. But none of these eight individuals views him or herself as heroic. In fact, all of them face a double disgrace in the eyes of society: they made what many would view as a cowardly attempt on their lives, and they failed in the process.

Shame and humiliation present major emotional barriers to overcome in the aftermath of a suicide attempt. This compounds and compromises the healing process for damaged bodies and devastated egos. Nearly eight years after his failed suicide attempt, one individual still referred to himself as "damaged goods." Toppled from a position of prominence, he is now engaged in the ignominious process of putting his life back together, piece by excruciating piece. He declined to be included in this project, preferring that his suicide attempt remain out of the spotlight until he had accomplished more of the healing process.

In his book, *Transforming Depression,* psychiatrist David Rosen recognizes the potential for transformation offered by the psychological crisis of suicidal depression. He explores the other side of the suicide coin, showing how this self-destructive threat may actually affirm a capacity to discover what he calls a "meaningful alternative to suicide."

Rosen's thesis grew out of his own experiences with depression and was further delineated by his professional therapy practice and research on individuals who survived suicidal leaps off the Golden Gate and San Francisco-Oakland Bay Bridges. In his book, Rosen describes the healing journey facing those who confront suicidal depression as a symbolic transcendence of death and transforming rebirth: "Each of them was involved in a journey toward wholeness that was related to a cycle of living and symbolically dying, and living again, which is the antithesis to the ego's ultimate claim to control, i.e., suicide."

Transcendence and transformation may be appropriate tools for understanding the healing process faced by these eight survivors as well. A creative, life-affirming dimension of the healing journey is confirmed by similarities in those resources they have used to mend their broken lives. Their divergent experiences with therapy and social support also reveal striking parallels. But the differences in their paths toward wholeness hold the real value. For they represent alternatives for coping with the challenge of survival and illustrate a variety of creative affirmations that support the reason for and result of living life more fully. And the more options there are to identify with resources for rebound and repair, the more effective and lasting will be the healing.

Most books on suicide seem to be designed primarily for a professional audience as a guide to therapeutic intervention and research. Fragmented anecdotes and brief vignettes are often interspersed with theoretical constructs and statistical studies, all in an effort to provide an understanding of how people fall into acute suicidal crisis, and then how they begin the healing process.

As valuable as this literature is for therapists and researchers, however, it is difficult for those contemplating suicide or recovering from an attempt, or even those in the individual's support system, to identify with such fragmented stories of different people at different stages of recovery. With few exceptions, there is an absence in the literature of complete stories told by ordinary people as they explore their experiences and discover how to live their lives more fully in the aftermath of suicidal despair.

This book is an attempt to fill this gap. It focuses only on a few people, but in much more depth. Their stories are offered free from theoretical or empirical constraints. Through them readers vicariously feel their determination to persevere; they cheer them on as they reaffirm their commitment to living and work to give their lives new value and purpose.

The three men and five women chosen for the book constitute a diverse group from varying walks of life with vastly different resources. Their suicide attempts occurred at different ages and different stages in life, and at least ten years has elapsed since the occurrence of each. This period, which in the longest case is more than twenty years, was a time of recovery.

For all it was necessary to allow enough insight and stability to fully reflect on the course of their lives before and after their attempts.

None of these individuals have been patients of the author. They were met for the first time well into their process of recovery, which allowed more objectivity than if the author were intimately involved in the healing process. The suicide attempts of these individuals provide a common bond for this group of eight, a starting point for their healing stories to begin. But these personal reflections are more about facing life than about seeking death through suicide. Their stories tell us more about the pattern and texture of their lives than they do about the final product.

For Josie, a suicide attempt is intricately woven into the fabric of physical and sexual abuse in childhood, a troubled youth of gang violence and institutional neglect, and a young motherhood for which she was unprepared.

Paul's story reveals the poignant reflections of an energetically creative actor and writer. His suicidal overdose was just a small slice of a much larger life of risk-taking as a gay alcoholic living in an intolerant society.

Mary's leap from a bridge at the age of eighteen left her paralyzed from the waist down, confined to a wheelchair and in chronic pain. For this world-class distance runner it could have been a fate worse than death. But her story has allowed Mary to reach out to others as a counselor in training, giving new meaning and purpose to her life in the process.

Risk-taking in Pam's life involved extensive drug use and self-mutilation, which affected her efforts to develop a healthy and lasting relationship. It culminated in an attempt to hang herself at the age of twenty-seven. She, too, survived to help others who have faced similar crises in their lives.

Frank has overcome a family legacy of completed suicides as well as his own self-destructive alcoholism. His recovery has hinged upon ten committed years in Alcoholics

6

Anonymous and a willingness to take more responsible risks to repair his psychological wounds.

Ken's training as a psychiatrist did not prevent him from falling into a self-destructive pattern of drug abuse and suicidal overdoses. His healing journey has meant creatively weaving his experiences into a more effective method of reaching out to help others.

Martha's story involves the devastating impact of her mother committing suicide when Martha was twelve years of age. By the age of fifteen, she would begin her own series of suicide attempts but, unlike her mother, would fail each time. By using her artistic creativity and learning to nurture herself, Martha has forged a new life of meaning and purpose.

It was an overdose in a lonely hotel room nearly twenty years ago that jump-started Sharon's healing process. Through a series of self-created challenges and opportunities, Sharon has come to terms with her complex relationships with family and friends. She continues the process of solidifying her resilience and determination to live life more fully and effectively.

It is important to note that all of these individuals were selected based on their willingness to share their experiences. Some protection has been provided by using only first names and disguising certain circumstances, but the events of their lives are as they have presented them. Hours of face-to-face interviews were supplemented with follow-up contacts to organize, clarify, and expand the material.

These stories of healing reflect each individual's ongoing struggle to survive lives full of complicated choices and potential potholes on the road to recovery. It is impossible to know how these eight individuals differ from those who are successful in completing their suicides, but it is clear that they have invaluable and inspiring lessons to teach. Their survival presents the unique opportunity to learn more about life and about death. These personal stories, filled with special understanding and penetrating insight, are mirrors into a past filled with pain and despair. Yet they offer glimpses of a more hopeful future. If we listen carefully, we may be better prepared to deal with our own contemplations of suicide, better prepared to help and support those who face depression and suicidal crisis, and better prepared to live our lives with renewed meaning, purpose, and commitment.

2

And Then There Were Angels

Flickering sunlight streamed through the stained glass windows, gently bathing the plush maroon carpet. A rainbow of colors danced in the aisles of St. Thomas Aquinas Catholic Church in the Bronx. Through her tears, Josie surveyed the faceless people arrayed in the pews before her. Their heads were turned toward the altar as she stood in the back of the church awaiting the signal to begin the wedding processional.

This was the special day she and Garry had carefully planned for many months. They obsessed over every detail: the shiny white Rolls Royce, the flowers, the music, the three-layered wedding cake, the champagne, and the reception planned for the community room. Family and friends brought heaping containers of chicken, rice, potato salad, macaroni and cheese, collard greens, and black-eyed peas.

Although the guest list was intentionally small, the most important people in Josie's life were all there. Her youngest daughter, Latoya, looked radiantly beautiful as the flower girl. Her son, also named Garry, nervously took charge of bearing the ring. Josie's three other children, Ebony, Deasean, and Latanya, also took part in the ceremony, along with four bridesmaids and her matron of honor, Michelle.

Gazing over the heads bobbing in the pews, Josie spotted the tight gray curls of her adoptive mother, Clara. She sat rigidly toward the front of the church. Although Clara's compliments were rarely elicited, Josie somehow knew that her adoptive mother was proud of her for arranging the whole wedding completely on her own. "She didn't put a dime in my way," Josie would explain when discussing her stepmother's lack of involvement in the wedding plans. She had become accustomed to Clara's withholding and learned to be suspicious of her infrequent expressions of love, especially since they often emerged only after violent episodes of abuse which occurred during periods of drunken rage. "When she used to tell me she loved me, it be after she done beat the crap out of me," Josie recalls painfully. She vividly remembers the sting of the ironing cord and the burning pain of the belt buckle striking her skin.

More hurtful than the physical abuse, however, were the long, lonely stretches of being locked in a closet, a punishment of dark and solitary confinement for her failure to complete homework. And then there was the verbal abuse. Stinging tirades savaged Josie's fragile self-esteem as she struggled to grow up in a troubled world. Josie recalls Clara's most frequent description of her: stupid bitch. But her stepmother added insult to injury when she would pronounce, "You're always going to be a stupid bitch."

Looking back, Josie understands the wounds Clara's angry words left on her. "Emotionally, stuff like that can affect a child very badly," Josie explains. "People don't realize . . .

10

emotional abuse—mental abuse—that hurts even more, you know. You tell a child you're not going to be nothing, you're not going to be no good. That hurts just as much as beating them. It hurts, it really does."

Josie could feel the hurt deep within her gut. The tears of joy streaming down her cheeks on this, her wedding day, were mixed with the memory of a more frequent and familiar companion over the years, tortured pain. This pain had become the only emotional experience upon which she could truly depend. Strangely, Josie learned to trust it to meet her needs for stimulation, solace, attention. At times, the pain allowed for the illusion of control in a world where she struggled to stay afloat and simply survive.

Self-abuse began for Josie at the age of six when she used pins to prick and scratch her arms until they bled. She soon progressed to slicing her arms with razor blades. These sessions of self-inflicted pain occurred most frequently after verbally abusive encounters with Clara. When Clara wanted to hurt her more than such physical punishment could accomplish, she would say, "You're going to be just like your mother."

"I was what you call a 'trick baby,' so I have no father," Josie explains in her own unique way, dismissing her natural father as an unknown. Her mother, Doris, was a prostitute and a junkie whose four children were all removed by social services after years of neglect and a long history of drug abuse. As a heroin-addicted baby, Josie spent the first three months of her life in the hospital before she was adopted by Clara. The adoption, in fact, was never legalized but was "more or less a favor," Josie explains, based upon Clara's friendship with Doris. Clara's own daughter, Brenda, who was several years older than Josie, was an alcoholic like her mother. Brenda died of cirrhosis at the age of thirty-eight.

Clara's husband, Raymond, was reportedly the most stable member of Josie's adoptive family. But he worked long hours and was often not at home to witness the abuse. Josie

11

remembers that Raymond was "very nice to me. When he would come home and he would see me with a black-and-blue eye, or busted lip, or whatever the case may be, or he seen me sitting in the corner looking all scared, he would ask me what happened, you know. He would go to Clara and say, 'Why would you do this? If you didn't want her, why take her?' And then they would get into a big argument and they would start fighting. You know, it was a big complication. No matter which way you looked at it, it was problems."

In her thirty-five young years, Josie witnessed a host of traumas, all of which left indelible scars on her body and her impressionable mind. To this day, she experiences flashbacks of being raped by her older brother. She was eleven and he was sixteen at the time. Josie also remembers trying, unsuccessfully, to convince her stepmother that her brother had sexually molested her. Clara vehemently argued with her, "Your brother wouldn't do nothing like that to you because that's your brother. He loves you."

Another trauma occurred a few years later when she went to visit her natural mother. As a battle-hardened fourteen-year-old, Josie tracked her down through the neighborhood grapevine. She found her frail mother, Doris, sitting in the bathroom of a squalid apartment, a needle jutting from her track-scarred arm. As if she were appearing in a scripted nightmare, Josie vividly recalls a faceless man at the scene. There, in her mother's apartment, this man attempted to rape her while her mother watched passively, semiconscious from the heroin surging through her veins. "Please, Mommy, help me!" Josie remembers crying aloud, but to no avail.

Josie has continued to question her compelling desire to contact her mother, particularly in light of the traumatic abuse she suffered at the hands of the faceless man. She perceives it as a search for herself, a quest to define her own identity and understand her propensity for self-abuse. "Why was I there?" Josie asks plaintively. She answers quickly, reflecting a vulnerable innocence that belies her tough facade. "Because I was hoping for her to reach out to me. I'm looking at things like, okay, she had her problems. Everybody had their problems. I'm not the type of person to judge no one. I'm in no situation to judge nobody. I'm looking at it as, this is my mother, you know. I want to get to know her no matter what type of problems she had. I want to get to know Doris as Doris, okay,? Whether she's a junkie, whether she's an alcoholic, I want to get to know her."

Josie paused briefly to consider the unanswered questions that remain. "You know, maybe I can find out why she's into drugs. You know, maybe she was abused as a child and maybe we could get to know each other and try to help each other. I'm not saying I was looking for love and affection, because here I'm already fourteen, fifteen years old. I don't think you can really give me that type of love and affection. But just knowing that you're there, trying to have at least a friendship, you know. If nothing else, just to know that you're my mother and I can come and see you when I want to come and see you."

With the erosion of Josie's trust came anger. Her deep-seated rage boiled to the surface with the same intensity as the hurt and pain she had struggled to suppress. Waiting nervously in the back of the church on her wedding day, Josie caught a glimpse of herself mirrored in the glass door. She had chosen the dress carefully. The supple cut of the bodice accentuated the soft curves of her ample frame. The long white sleeves covered most of the pink scars which were still visible on the black skin of her wrists and arms. She knew that the years of self-abuse—the scratching and slicing with pins and razors—were a misguided effort to keep her anger from erupting toward others. She also knew that the self-inflicted pain was exhilarating, an adrenaline rush which strangely made her feel powerful at a time when she was emotionally battered. And at the same time, it was a transparent, and ultimately unsuccessful, attempt to get love and attention from her adoptive mother.

"I had a lot of anger," Josie recalls. "I had a lot of anger. And I used to feel that all I wanted was to be loved. You know? And a lot of times I feel I was doing it out of attention. I wanted this woman to love me, not to keep abusing me. And a lot of times when she would see my arms scratched up she would say, 'Just go in the bathroom and wash it off.' You know, it wouldn't be like she would care."

The rage within Josie was not fully contained by her self-mutilation, however. As she navigated the troubled waters of her teenage years, Josie's anger began to erupt more forcefully and more often. At times her fury was frightening and explosively violent. She became the victimizer rather than the victim. She discovered her capacity and her power to inflict pain on others in order to protect herself. Fueled by this intimidating rage and intense need for acceptance, Josie joined with other disaffected youth to form neighborhood gangs with benign and esoteric names such as the Seven Crowns and the Black Spades. She carried a knife and was not afraid to use it for self-defense or to avenge another gang member.

Josie's violent fighting soon brought her to the attention of the police, who arrested her on a number of occasions. Beginning at the age of fifteen, she was incarcerated in a series of group homes and juvenile detention facilities. Such institutional placements severely disrupted her education. Josie failed to complete the eighth grade when she was expelled for a fight with school security guards. "The police came, and they tried to sedate me by holding me down. I started fighting and acting wild with them, and they took a blackjack and busted me upside my head two or three times and busted my skull, you know. But to the judge it didn't make a difference because I was violent to them. I was trying to hurt them, so they had to restrain me."

Josie's violent rage against the world survived her

turbulent teenage years and continued well into her twenties. She recalls a particularly explosive fourth of July as a young adult when she got into a fight with a man at the train station. He approached her brandishing a crowbar, accusing her of stealing money from him. "So he had a crowbar in his hand and everybody say, 'Run, run!' So I, like, stood right there, because if I run I might get messed up even worse. So as I stood there, he took the crowbar, he swung it at me, and he hit me in my head. So I picked up a bottle and broke it. And when he swung and hit me, for some reason I felt like the Incredible Hulk. . . . When you angry, you get a lot of hostility. You get this incredible strength." Using the sharp edge of the broken bottle, Josie inflicted massive damage to the man's arm which later required nearly forty stitches. Although the police arrested Josie at the scene, she was released from jail two days later when the man refused to press charges.

Josie realizes now that her explosive anger directed toward the world was her way of defending against the hurt and pain she had endured throughout her young life. It was a means of protecting the fragile, wounded child who lived within her, the child who continued to search for the good mother with the loving care she most desperately needed. Josie is also aware that her self-mutilation was an impulsive reflection of this angry, hurt child, but not an attempt to kill herself. Self-destructive and self-abusive, certainly, but in her mind she knows this was not suicidal behavior.

Suicide for Josie was not a planned event. The urge seemed to creep up on her, catching her off guard. She recalls the multiple episodes of impulsive overdose with aspirin which made her sick. She also remembers ingesting poisons—rat poison and lye mixed with Kool-aid—which got her admitted to the hospital emergency room. According to Josie, these were impulsive, almost accidental, events, devoid of deliberation or even delay between thought and action. "I wouldn't think about it," Josie recalls. "I would just do it. My

15

reaction to suicide was I'd just do it right then and there. . . . I don't think about the consequences."

Blindness in her right eye and residual pain from her broken pelvis serve as constant reminders of Josie's most serious suicide attempt. She was only twenty-two when she jumped from the window of her fourth-floor apartment. The emotional trigger for this death-defying fall remains a blur as she attempts to recall it years later. She vaguely remembers Clara grabbing her by the neck, pushing her up against the wall, and smacking her in the face. She remembers those familiar searing words that ripped through her, hurting worse than the physical pain: "You stupid bitch. You worthless nothing." Josie explains, "She got me very angry, you know. The things she said really hurt me. I started crying, telling her, 'I love you, Mommy. Why are you saying this?' She said, 'I don't love you. I don't care nothing about you, you this, you that.' And I said, 'Screw it. If I wasn't here, I wouldn't have to go through this.'"

With the same detached numbness that accompanied the slicing of her arms with razor blades, Josie suddenly found herself sitting on the edge of the windowsill, looking down four stories to the alley below. She remembers a girlfriend telling her from the window of another apartment across the alley, "No, Josie, don't do this. It's not worth it. You have a long life ahead of you. You have your children." But Josie's impulses kept her fixated on the compulsion to do it and get it over with. "I'm saying, no I want to die," she recalls. "I don't want to be here no more. I'm sick and tired of this bullshit."

She remembers her oldest daughter, age five at the time, trying to grab her hand in an attempt to pull her back as she hung from the edge of the window ledge. The touch of her daughter's hand seemed to shock Josie back to the reality of what was happening. Her ambivalence about dying suddenly kicked in, interrupting her intention to let go. "No, Mommy, no," her daughter pleaded, reminding her of her own plaintive cries at Clara's abuse. The sound of her daughter's voice and the touch of her small hand were too late to save Josie from falling, however. Struggling to climb back in the window, while at the same time pushing her daughter away, Josie lost her grip and fell accidentally.

She lost consciousness when her face hit the street. Her skull fractured, her pelvis broken, and her sight impaired, Josie remained in intensive care for two weeks. She has forgotten much about her hospitalization, but she remembers envisioning angels—delicate white figures with wings, flying around her as if in a dream. Thinking back, Josie understands this dream state as the near-death experience that occurred between when her heart stopped beating and when the doctors revived her. "They had to put the machine on me to pump me back," she explains. "You know, people don't believe me, but when I was going that few seconds, I saw angels and I guess those angels must have brought me back. . . . While I was dead I saw these angels."

Josie has never considered herself to be an especially religious or spiritual person. In fact, there was a time when she questioned her belief in a deity of any kind. "Okay, because I looked at it as, if there was a God, why did I have to go through the type of abuse that I went through? Somebody up there should've helped me a long time ago. Why help me when I fell out the window? I wanted the help long, long ago. I needed the help back then."

Despite her questioning of a protective and benevolent God, Josie found herself believing in the guardian angels who were there to bring her back from the grip of death. One of these angels later turned out to be the man who stood at the front of the church on her wedding day, patiently waiting for her to walk down the aisle.

Josie met Garry the day before she fell from the window. At first, she thought he was like most men who get what they want in a one-night stand and are never seen again. But Garry turned out to be different. He came to see her the next day. When a neighbor told him about Josie's accident, he visited her in the hospital. Two weeks later when she awoke from her coma, Garry was there by her side, patiently supporting her, encouraging her to continue fighting, pleading with her not to give up. Garry became the director in Josie's second chance at life, helping to orchestrate the healing process that brought her back from the brink of death.

It took several years before Josie could begin to trust Garry enough to tell him about her life prior to her suicide attempt. Sexual intimacy provided the medium for defining Josie's history of pain and betrayal, as well as a platform for rebuilding her sense of trust. Flashbacks of being raped invaded their intimacy, eliciting anger and defensiveness in Josie. But Garry persevered. With patience and understanding, he helped Josie to gradually open up and relate her feelings and experiences.

Garry listened. He did not judge her, as Josie had been conditioned to expect. Instead, he shared the anger she still felt toward her brother and the love-hate relationship she had with her adoptive mother. Garry supported Josie's efforts to put the past behind her and create a more healthy, open relationship between them. He was there to help her through her episodes of self-abuse as well. "A lot of times he's seen me cut up my arms, and a lot of times he'll bandage me up. He's in the National Guard and they teach them first aid. To prevent me going to the hospital and the cops getting involved— because, you know, when you're suicidal, the cops come and . . . they might want to take the children—to prevent that, he used to bandage me up, stitch my arm up, and stuff like that. So a lot of times, he did it, and after he finished I would talk. . . . Eventually I would come and tell him what was the problem."

Over the years their relationship gradually developed, and trust and openness strengthened. In addition to her son and daughter, Josie and Garry had three more children. Josie's oldest was fathered by a man she met during one of her hospitalizations. "He treated me nice for a while," she recalls. "We decided when we got out of the hospital we would live together. We found an apartment, and that's when the abuse started." When money ran low for food, they resorted to panhandling on the streets. But Josie drew the line when it became clear that he expected her to prostitute herself for money. "We ran out of money again, and he asked me how much I loved him. I told him again I loved him a whole lot, so he said if I loved him I would wear this pair of very tight see-through shorts and go out on the streets and sell my body for money. I told him I didn't love him that much, so he took a baseball bat and beat me in the back of my head."

Forty-three stitches later, the doctor in the emergency room told Josie that she was pregnant. She did not return to the abusive boyfriend, but decided to keep the baby. "I needed someone to love me and I needed someone to love," Josie explains.

Life on the streets for a single pregnant woman was difficult. Before Josie was able to get on welfare and find an apartment, she found herself sleeping in abandoned buildings, on trains, and on the streets. When she finally gave birth to Latanya, the Bureau of Child Welfare questioned her ability to take care of the baby and threatened to take her away. Eventually she and her child were released from the hospital together, and Josie was faced with the demands of being a new mother on her own.

With motherhood, Josie was confronted with the dilemma of all abuse survivors who become parents themselves. Would the pattern of abuse be passed on to the next generation? Or would she be capable of eradicating the abuse? Could she protect her children from growing up hurt, angry, and confused? Josie recognizes now that striving to become a more effective and loving mother was an essential part of her own healing process.

This process of learning to parent has forced Josie to confront a powerful urge to physically and verbally abuse her children. She vividly recalls a scene when she angrily pushed her daughter's head into a sink full of water because she would not hold still while she was washing her hair. When Josie became aware of what she was doing, she quickly retreated to her room. Turning her anger toward herself, she began cutting her arms in the perpetual self-punishing ritual she had learned to depend on for comfort and control. But even her self-punishment could not stop the cycle of abuse. Confronting the violent rage within her has been and will forever be a struggle for Josie. It is the legacy of a childhood of abuse.

The culmination of Josie's years of pain and anguish occurred during one of her pregnancies. She swallowed lye in an attempt to end her life. Looking back, she now realizes that was dangerous not only to herself but also to her unborn child. It is difficult for her to rationalize the horror of the act, but she knows that her thought processes were distorted at that period in her life; her impulse control was practically nonexistent. "I wasn't thinking of the consequences on the baby," Josie explains. "I was thinking of the consequences on myself, killing myself, and feeling that it won't damage the baby. The baby will be fine. And now I look back and I was, like . . . damn, you know what I'm saying? I could have really killed my child."

An important part of Josie's recovery has been her involvement in therapy with a doctor she learned to trust. Dr. B seemed different from the other doctors Josie had dealt with over the years. "He listened to me," she says. "He waited 'til I was ready to open up, to share my story with him. He didn't judge me. He didn't lock me up. He didn't dope me with medication."

Josie's distrust of doctors was largely the result of many years of involuntarily confinement in psychiatric hospitals where she was frequently drugged with powerful sedatives. The drugs left her calm but confused, less of a threat to herself and others. But at the same time, they left her helpless to reach out and communicate the insurmountable pain she was feeling. "Maybe they had their reasons," Josie rationalizes. "When I came into a lot of hospitals, I was a very violent, hyperactive child. So maybe that was their way of calming me down. You know, then I wasn't a talkative person. I didn't talk."

Talking has become Josie's primary resource for a healthy way of thinking about the world. Talking serves to delay the destructive impulses long enough for her to regain control. With more control, she is able to reconnect with her children, her husband, her friends, and her doctor. Dr. B, described as "an African-American with a beard and a funny white hat," treats Josie in individual sessions and also sees the children in family therapy. For the past ten years, Dr. B has been an important anchor for Josie, helping her learn to talk to her kids rather than act out in pain and anger.

"I have this rocking chair, and I sit and I rock," Josie describes what she calls "flashbacks" of abuse. "And when I get like that, my children will come to me and say, 'Mommy, you okay?' Because they'll feel that I'm going into these deep thoughts, and I'll get depressed and I might try to hurt myself again. I tried it in front of my children. That I will never, as long as I live, do again in front of them. My oldest daughter had this fear of me going near the window because she saw me when I fell out the window. So I more or less informed them, 'No, Mommy's not going to hurt herself. Mommy's just upset because she's thinking about what Grandma did or what my brother did to me.'"

Josie is not afraid to talk about her experiences openly and honestly with her children. Although there are times she worries about her children becoming depressed or suicidal themselves, she feels it is important that they know what she has experienced in her life. She hopes this openness will give

21

them permission to talk about their own anger and pain, their own fears and worries.

Josie has discovered that her ability to be open in talking about her life can be helpful to others as well. For the past three years, Josie has been actively involved in giving community workshop presentations on suicide, child abuse, and domestic violence. Through a nonprofit educational organization, Josie has shared her story of traumatic physical and emotional abuse and her personal experience with suicidal depression. Sometimes Josie talks one-to-one with kids. At other times she may give a presentation to a large group of students, teachers, or counselors. Whenever she presents, she talks straight from her heart, drawing from the insight she has gained in confronting her anger and pain, putting her feelings into words rather than perpetually acting them out in a self-defeating cycle of abuse.

"You know, I get a lot of crying, 'cause it's very emotional," Josie explains. "I get a lot of crying from the audience. I get a lot of questions. Some of them have been through attempts at suicide, but they don't have nobody they can talk to because nobody wants to believe them, you know. So I feel when kids hear somebody else who's been through it, and they see that person is getting better, that gives them a chance to share and open up."

Through that openness and sharing Josie has learned that she helps herself by helping others. It helps her to stay in touch with the anger and pain that persist within her, remnants of the slowly healing wound of physical and emotional abuse. It helps her immensely to feel the compassion and understanding emanating from those who hear her story and identify with her experiences. And it helps her in her process of developing a new part of her identity—that of the caring counselor who can touch the hurt and anger in others and become a facilitator of their own healing process.

"I'm a caring person. I love people," Josie explains with

renewed insight. Through her workshop presentations, she has discovered how important it is to simply listen to what people have to say without judging them, without telling them what to feel or what not to feel. "A lot of times when I used to be at home and I felt suicidal," she recalls, "I used to pick up the phone and I used to call the hotline numbers. And by them letting me talk and them listening to me, it helped. . . . That was when I got to the age where I felt I needed help. . . . And sometimes I would be on the phone for hours, you know, and they just hear me out, you know, and it feels good, you know, to just hear somebody out and not to judge them."

Josie aspires to be a counselor one day, to help children deal with the difficulties of growing up in a world where domestic violence, physical and sexual abuse, and suicidal depression are everyday realities. But she worries that her lack of proper schooling will hold her back from gaining the degree she needs to become a social worker. Josie is not sure she has the patience and stamina to pick up where she left off in the eighth grade and persist through the many years of academic work necessary to obtain her degree.

"You have to have a certain amount of education to really deal with children, I'm sure." Josie explains, "I have the knowledge as far as being through abusive things that they might go through and how to talk to them and help them to deal with it, but as far as doctors and social workers, I don't have that. I have to go to school to be a social worker. . . . I wouldn't mind working in group homes, you know what I'm saying. That, you know, I'm dealing with children and I'm helping other kids, you know. I love to help people. I give my heart out to a person, you know. I always get messed up in the process, but I give my heart out to people."

Josie does not expect everyone to understand her heartfelt honesty and openness. In fact, she is prepared to be rejected in the process of trying to reach out and help people. But she is more confident than ever before that she will not become her own worst enemy, falling back into despair. Josie is insistent that her self-control is intact, that her suicidal impulses are in check. Her distrust and anger remain, but they now function as her protection rather than a weapon. "I'm not going to fall back no more . . . for the sake of my children. As far as being suicidal . . . it did too much damage to my children . . . and I'm not going to see my children emotionally disturbed.

"I have a lot to live for now, especially my children, especially helping other people," Josie continues, expressing a more resolute empathy, a more determined sense of self. "I don't want anybody looking at me and saying, 'I knew that lady. She came and did a workshop and she told us all this and look what she did to herself; she killed herself.' You know what I'm saying? No, I don't want that. I'm not going to contradict myself like that. I done reached out to so many people and hopefully I'm helping other people in the process of helping myself also. Because this is also a healing process for me to come out and share my story with other people, you know. The more I talk about it, the more it helps me. You know, people don't realize when you talk a lot about things that bother you it helps. It's not going to help and go away right away. But it helps."

Josie pauses to reflect on her own struggle to help herself, acknowledging the exceedingly slow healing process. "Sometimes I get mad at myself because I have to look at my arms."

On the day of her wedding, Josie was careful to hide the scars on her arms by the long sleeves of her wedding gown. The healing process at this stage in her life was far from complete, but her wedding day was to be a celebration of determined resolution and renewed commitment. It was to be a day for healing old wounds and beginning a new lease on life. Josie would celebrate her new identity as a wife for the first time, but also as a more healthy and more complete mother. She was determined to work hard to overcome the legacy of abuse which was her birthright, passed along from her natural mother, Doris, to her alcoholic and abusive adoptive mother, Clara.

Josie's wedding day represented a significant turning point, a defining event in her tempestuous emotional journey from its start as an abused child who grew up to be an abusive parent to its ultimate goal as a mother capable of caring for herself as well as her children. In the end, this healing journey would lead even farther, transforming her from a self-abusing, suicidal victim crying out for help to a caring counselor who reaches out to help others struggling with their own anger and pain.

Just as her wedding day offered Josie a new beginning on her emotional journey to find herself, she faced another significant turning point when her adoptive mother died. It was in July, shortly after her fourth wedding anniversary, when her adoptive father, Raymond, told her of Clara's illness. Clara had been sick for a number of weeks—not eating and losing weight, but still drinking heavily. Her cirrhotic liver was rapidly shutting down, the product of years of alcohol abuse, but Clara stubbornly refused to see a doctor or go to the hospital. Raymond implored Josie to help him convince Clara to go to the hospital. When Josie arrived at the apartment, she found her adoptive mother lying in bed, painfully thin and disoriented, unable to distinguish who Josie was. Clara referred to Josie as Brenda, her natural born daughter who had died some years earlier from cirrhosis of the liver.

Despite the years of emotional and physical abuse and her efforts to maintain some protective distance from her adoptive mother, Josie could never give up her love for her. "I would never disown her," Josie assures adamantly. "If anything would happen to her, I would go to her and help her." She recalls Clara's own words of assurance that Josie and her children would be taken care of financially if she were to die. "You and the kids going to be well off. You ain't never going to want for nothing," Clara had said.

A glimpse of Josie's resentment emerges as she reflects the understanding she developed about her adoptive mother's efforts to be a good provider and a "good grandma" during her last years of life. "It was more or less like she wanted to give me—now that she was gone—what she didn't want to give me back then. But I don't want it now. All I want from her is the love and affection that I always wanted and still was trying to get before she died."

Josie remembers helping the emergency medical technicians carefully lift Clara's limp body into the ambulance, feeling the sharp edges of Clara's bones protruding through her parchment-thin skin. She had visited her every day in the hospital and even seemed hopeful that she was getting better. She remembers praying that Clara would recover and return home.

And she remembers the night Clara died. She had pleaded with the security guard to allow her to see her adoptive mother one last time. "And I remember crying and I remember hugging her. . . . She was just laying there. And I just hugged her and told her, 'Mommy, I love you.' And I kept saying, 'Mommy, I love you. Mommy, I love you.' And I remember saying, 'Please come back, Mommy. Please come back. Please don't leave me.'"

As Josie recalls Clara's death, she reexperiences the abandonment she has suffered her whole life. At the same time, Josie remembers that Clara's death enabled her to shed a large piece of that painful childhood. The child that was huddled in the dark corners of her mind would now have to learn to mother herself in a healthier, more determined way. This child would grow up to be an adult who could learn to parent her own children, to meet her own needs through a good marriage, and to reach out as a caring counselor helping others with their own suffering.

Josie remembers Clara's funeral: the casket was open; her

hair was perfectly set; and she was wearing the same green dress she had worn to Josie's wedding. Josie's tears had been mixed with feelings of renewed strength and determination—the strength to face life on her own with new meaning and purpose, and the determination to persist no matter what obstacles got in her way.

As Josie had quietly stood near Clara's body resting in the casket, she could feel the years of hurt and anger released through her tears. She had been able to remember the simple words of prayer that Clara always repeated to her before bedtime: "Now I lay me down to sleep. I pray the Lord my soul to keep. If I should die before I wake, I pray the Lord my soul to take." Softly repeating this prayer to herself, Josie cried quietly.

3

The Show Must Go On

It was a warm June day when Angus died; a Thursday, Paul recalls. Angus would have been forty-seven if he had lived until November, when he and Paul had traditionally celebrated their birthdays together. Paul was ten years younger. He could take some small comfort in remembering his last visit: when he surprised Angus on his birthday. It happened to be Thanksgiving Day—another significant Thursday—when Paul boarded a morning flight from New York. He arrived in London earlier than anticipated. "It's as if even God smiled," Paul says sardonically, recalling the look of surprise on Angus's face when he suddenly appeared at his door.

They spent the weekend together. When Paul finally left, he thought he was seeing his friend for the last time. But Angus surprised him. They saw each other again the next spring when Paul flew over to run the London Marathon. When it came time to say good-bye, Angus had said, "I'll see you in the fall." But Paul knew this was to be the last time he would see his friend alive.

Angus had lived too long, Paul thought, immediately recoiling at the harshness of the thought. Nevertheless, he knew it was true. Or perhaps it was just that the process of dying seemed to drag on excessively. Angus lived a tortured existence the entire last year of his life. Paul remembers Angus laying in bed for months as the parade of opportunistic infections took turns ravaging his weary, beaten-down body. The AIDS virus had begun the war by obliterating Angus's immune system, but the infections insidiously finished him off. Names of these foreign invaders sound like a cast of alien characters from a galactic war script: toxoplasmosis, cryptosporidiosis, and pneumocystis carinii.

"The last year of his life was horrific," Paul concludes. While there probably is no "good death," dying from AIDS is a particularly gruesome way to go. Of all the friends and acquaintances Paul has known over the years who have died from the devastating effects of AIDS, Angus's death was the most difficult for him to endure.

"I've never been as close to anyone in my life. He was my closest friend. He was the closest I've ever had to a brother. He's the person I loved the most in my life." Yet, he and Angus were so dissimilar in their personalities. Paul was an outgoing and effusive Englishman. Angus, a quiet Scot, was exceedingly shy and reserved. Somehow their relationship worked despite their differences.

They shared so many interests within the arts: galleries, opera, theater, modern dance. Their creative energy overlapped as well, although directed into different artistic mediums. Paul is an accomplished actor and writer. Angus was recognized as one of Britain's leading potters. Paul fondly describes his friend as a "bizarre potter" whose sculptured ceramics were heavily influenced by the bright color schemes of Central and Latin America. Angus's work was widely exhibited in Europe.

Reviewers frequently commented about the impact of HIV on Angus's later work. In fact, it was their shared HIV positive status that initially brought Paul and Angus together many years earlier. When Paul was first diagnosed in 1984, authorities referred to this mysterious virus as the human T-cell lymphotropic virus, or HTLV-III, for short. Although it was believed then that only 10 percent of those who tested positive would go on to develop full-blown AIDS, the diagnosis hit Paul like a death sentence. He was fully aware that no effective treatment existed. Furthermore, he knew that life expectancy for someone with AIDS was predicted to be extremely short—generally eight months or less.

Diagnostic techniques for detecting antibodies to the AIDS virus were available, but Paul procrastinated. He recalls now that he later decided to get tested after a frightening nightmare that he was going to die of AIDS. During those early days of the AIDS epidemic, it took up to four weeks to get the results back. At the time, Paul had been acting in a weekly TV series, playing a Spock-like character in a children's science fiction show. Of slight build, Paul speaks with a crisp British accent. His resonating voice allowed him to project a strong, forceful persona that contrasted sharply with his youthful appearance. The combination was well-suited for the role.

He remembers being preoccupied with the impending test results, and recalls significant emotional stress during that time, stress that is evident in reviewing videotapes of the series. "I did not think I was positive; I did not know anyone who was," Paul says. "I did not know anyone personally who had died of AIDS, which meant, when it came back positive . . . Wow!"

A friend gave him a phone number and suggested he join a support group for people who were HIV positive. Following

31

rehearsals one day, Paul arranged to meet Jonathan, one of the founders of a group called Body Positive. Paul found the experience of getting to know someone living with the deadly virus profoundly therapeutic. "Simply to be in the same room with somebody else who was HIV positive, who was not dead or dying, and who was bright and intelligent, witty and funny . . . full of vigor . . . He's still alive today, I'm delighted to say."

As Paul reflects on his participation in the support group, he becomes painfully aware that very few of the original members are still alive. Of the four still living, he is one of the few who has not developed full-blown AIDS. Defusing strong emotions in a creatively light-hearted manner, Paul continues, "If I were to write a volume of autobiography, which I have no intention of doing, I'd call it 'Ten Green Bottles.' Over here you have this song for children called 'One Hundred Bottles of Beer on the Wall.' Well, the English version is shorter. It's a little more economical; it's called 'Ten Green Bottles.'" Paul breaks out in song, presenting a brief musical rendition in a lilting tenor:

> Ten green bottles standing on the wall.
> Ten green bottles standing on the wall.
> And if one green bottle should accidentally fall,
> There'll be nine green bottles standing on the wall.

And all the way down to one. So I think I'd call it 'Four Green Bottles,' absolutely. And there aren't many green bottles left." Of course, the green bottle that mattered most to Paul was his friend Angus.

Approaching his first meeting of Body Positive, Paul was "petrified." He was exceedingly anxious about who was going to be there and how he would relate to these other HIV "victims." He met Angus at that first meeting, "a rather quiet Scot in a sports jacket," Paul recalls. "I didn't find him the least bit attractive really. Nice, pleasant, charming. Two weeks later, the support group met again. He was there again. Polite conversation and, you know, the last thing that crossed my mind was that we were going to wind up having a relationship together. We were very unlike. He hated crowds, hated meeting people he didn't know."

At the time, Angus was still mourning the death of his lover who had been one of the first people in England to die of AIDS. Perhaps this unresolved loss was one of the reasons Paul and Angus had difficulty as lovers. The looming threat of AIDS hung over them both, a constant reminder that life is temporary.

"Neither of us planned to have a relationship with anybody," Paul explains. "I honestly thought my life was imperiled. The last thing I was thinking about was starting to have a relationship with somebody—the last thing. I also felt I would probably never ever have sex again with anyone. I thought my sex life was over. Until this support group, I didn't know people who were HIV positive."

Paul stops for a moment to reflect, then continues his reminiscence of Angus. "I remember the first time we slept together, it was like two live hand grenades. in bed. We weren't altogether totally sure what one could and could not do. I don't make this out to sound like the Stone Age, but, in terms of HIV, it was. This was very early on."

The relationship that developed between Paul and Angus was immensely more successful as a close friendship than a romantic relationship. They lived separately but spent a great deal of time together. In addition to enjoying long drives in the country, they shared dinners at intriguing restaurants and explored their common interests in the performing arts. After Paul moved to New York five years ago, their relationship continued to deepen through regularly scheduled and eagerly anticipated visits. On occasion, Paul flew over to London simply to spend a weekend with Angus.

Their HIV status initially brought them together. But over

33

the course of their relationship, Paul realized that he and Angus held a significantly different outlook on life, a different attitude about their shared disease, and a different view of the future. While Paul viewed the AIDS virus as an enemy to be fought with all his might and will, Angus seemed resigned to a more passive and fateful view of life. Angus believed that he was destined to die and that fighting would not appreciably alter the outcome.

When news of Angus's death reached Paul in New York, he felt that a part of him had died as well. He was not shocked; he knew it was going to happen when he said good-bye to Angus in April. A funeral service was planned, and family members asked Paul to present the eulogy. Although he first considered the task too wrenching, Paul knew he had to do it for his friend. He would have been furious with himself if he had let Angus down during this last ceremony. He made a few notes to himself, but knew what he needed to say. In retrospect, Paul says he wouldn't change a word of his public farewell, his final tribute to the closest friend he had ever had, the person he had loved the most.

June 28 arrived in London, a sultry warm day for early summer. Paul recalls how cool it was in the nineteenth-century stone chapel at Golders Green, one of the largest cemeteries in North London. Nearly one hundred people were in attendance. Paul noted that Angus would have been uncomfortable with such a large crowd, but would have been more at ease knowing Paul was there as his buffer.

A secular service was planned in accordance with Angus's humanistic convictions. Music and poetry readings were selected to reflect his passion for the performing arts. The service opened with "Andaggio" from Mozart's *Clarinet Concerto*, recorded by the Vienna Symphony, Paul recalls. Later there were musical selections recorded by Jessye Norman and Marilyn Horne along with readings of W. H. Auden's poetry. The Anglican priest who had officiated at the committal for

Angus's lover ten years earlier was there to preside over this service.

Paul delivered the eulogy for his friend with all the mastery his years of acting could provide him. His tears could not be rehearsed, but such overwhelming grief did not betray the performance. He closed with a selection from Dylan Thomas entitled "And Death Shall Have No Dominion." Paul struggled to contain the painful emptiness welling up from deep inside as he heard his voice speak the poet's words amidst the hushed coolness of the chapel. "Though lovers be lost love shall not, and death shall have no dominion." The sharply defined memories of his friend and lover were indelibly etched in his mind despite their relatively short time together in life and in love.

As the last yellow rose was placed on the coffin, the lifeless body exited stage right as though following a scripted play. Paul could finally say good-bye to his friend. "Angus' death was the closest death to me that I've ever experienced," Paul reflects more than two years later. Despite his grief and the painful longing for a love that could never be replaced, however, Paul continues to believe that Angus had lived too long, recalling the last horrific year of his life.

"I wish Angus had died earlier. It sounds evil and wicked to say," Paul confesses, but "I wouldn't wish it on my worst enemy." It seems Angus felt the same way at one point. Several years before the two met at the HIV support group, Angus had attempted suicide through a drug overdose. "I don't know anybody who's HIV positive who hasn't thought about suicide," Paul ruefully concludes. He is somewhat surprised that more people with AIDS don't actually go through with it to escape the final tortured stage of their lives. Reflecting on his own thoughts about assisted suicide and the projected end of his own life, Paul admits, "It's crossed my mind that, looking ahead, it would be a very different suicide than the one I attempted."

To fully understand Paul's suicide attempt fifteen years earlier, it is important to note several significant dimensions of his life: the disapproval and shame of growing up as a gay young man in a conservative and traditional working class family, the pain and emptiness of envisioning a lonely life without a meaningful relationship, and the self-destruction of a drug and alcohol addiction that had been intensifying for years.

"I'd been working as an actor for nine months," Paul recalls the precursory circumstances of that critical period. "I'd gotten my equity card, and I had started drinking excessively. Relationships had been difficult to nonexistent. All I can say is, my life got darker and darker. And there didn't seem to be any light at the end of the tunnel. It was immediately after Christmas and I felt extremely lonely. I didn't see any prospect of my life getting better.

"It wasn't a cry for help, which I understand a lot of people attempt when they're trying to kill themselves. There was no intention of being found in time. I was down in the country. It was a house of a friend of mine which I used to visit. I'd spent Christmas down there and I just felt extremely, extremely, extremely depressed. And I got ahold of a drug. There's a drug in England, I don't know if it has the same brand name over here, called Mogadon. It's a sleeping tablet. I don't know how many I took . . . a couple dozen, and I'd been drinking heavily. I was drinking gin at the time. I remember being in this bedroom, toasting myself with gin for the last time and taking these tablets. It was a very old house, built around 1600, and I remember there was a mirror in the wardrobe door. I remember seeing myself in the mirror having toasted myself for the last time, and I was just delighted to be through with it. And I remember putting the glass down. I literally just slumped on the bed and that was it. I thought it was all over."

Paul has never been able to recover his own memories of the first few days following the overdose, but he has pieced together the sequence of events from talking with those who helped him through it. On his way to bed later that night, his friend happened to notice the light coming from under the door of Paul's room. He found Paul unconscious with the empty pill bottle nearby and summoned an ambulance to take him to the hospital.

Paul's first memory after losing consciousness is several days later when he was discharged from the hospital. He recalls being back in his friend's house, sitting in an armchair, eating scrambled eggs and toast. "That was my first memory," Paul declares. "I had no memory of anything in those days, absolutely nothing. Nothing's ever come back." He has been told that, during the forty-eight hours in the hospital, his stomach was pumped, he fell off a gurney, and he had an interview with a psychiatrist.

It was the light under the door that fateful night that inadvertently rescued Paul. It provided a spotlight for what he planned as the final and perhaps best performance of his short life—a desperately lonely actor on an empty stage. "If I hadn't left the light on," Paul notes, "there would have been no reason for suspicion to be aroused."

The suicide attempt left him feeling physically weak and emotionally fragile. Paul's first thought was that now everyone would know that he not only had tried to kill himself but had ingloriously failed in the attempt. "You see, I was doing a play at the time," he explains. "When I tried to kill myself, my last concern was that the play must go on—the show must go on and all that crap."

In the end, the show did go on for Paul. His suicide attempt survived public scrutiny, and he was able to continue his acting career. He was successful in a series of radio, television, film, and stage roles with a number of positive reviews over the years. Perhaps Paul's proudest acting accomplishment is his solo performance in a play he had written himself. It was a play about John Keats, the nineteenth-century British poet who died at the young age of twenty-five. His poetry reflected the profound sensuality of his imagination and the passionate vitality that characterized his short but productive life. Perhaps because of the premature death of family members, Keats had a premonition that death might shorten his writing career and prevent him from finding happiness in a romantic relationship. So when he developed a pulmonary hemorrhage, signaling an advanced stage of tuberculosis, Keats knew death was close at hand. In a poem simply entitled "On Death," Keats wrote:

> Can death be sleep when life is but a dream,
>   And scenes of bliss pass as a phantom by?
> The transient pleasures as a vision seem,
>   And yet we think the greatest pain's to die.
> How strange it is that man on earth should roam,
>   And lead a life of woe, but not forsake
> His rugged path; nor dare he view alone
>   His future doom which is but to awake.

In retrospect, Paul realizes that his writing this particular play about the life of Keats occurred during a critical period of transition in the mid-eighties. Paul was coming to terms with his HIV status for the first time and was gradually acknowledging the extent and impact of his alcoholism. The parallels between his own life and that of Keats would not become completely evident until some years later, after he had performed the play dozens of times in tours throughout Europe and the United States. "I did not sit down and say, 'This is going to be good therapy for me, to write a play about John Keats.' But what I ended up doing is writing a play, and then realizing that I'd picked a subject that I felt very close to."

Paul's success as an actor was threatened when his HIV status was announced publicly while he was playing one of the lead roles in the children's TV series. He remembers the national tabloid headline, "Children's TV Star in AIDS Scare." With his picture appearing on the front pages of the local London papers, Paul's private agony became public knowledge. With the carefully orchestrated support of his agent and friends, Paul was able to hold the journalists at bay with a firm "no comment." One friend in particular, an actor who had achieved a great deal of fame despite myriad personal problems of his own, was extraordinarily helpful to Paul during this critical period. When Paul verbalized his suicidal thoughts in the face of mounting pressure from the media, he recalled his friend's bold advice: "Don't let the bastards win."

"That's what carried me through," Paul wryly concludes, "don't let the bastards win." In a way, the "bastards" did win, however. Paul never had an audition with the British Broadcasting Corporation as an actor again. These were the early days in the history of AIDS—before Rock Hudson made his public announcement on his deathbed; before Magic Johnson, Arthur Ashe, and Gregg Louganis openly acknowledged their positive HIV status. The public's perception of HIV and AIDS carried with it a social stigma more condemning than the emotional scar Paul carried with him from his suicide attempt years earlier. He continued to act in plays and was becoming more effective in his writing, but Paul's TV series came to an abrupt end. He found himself facing a forlorn life, a life of severe restrictions in time, options, and opportunities.

His move to New York allowed him to regain some measure of privacy which he desperately needed to reorganize his priorities, and redirect his life and his work. By leaving England, Paul would be able to escape the media spotlight that haunted his career. But he would also be moving farther away from Angus. Paul knew he needed to make this sacrifice in order to regain some control over his life and felt confident that their special friendship would endure the distance.

Moving to New York also meant leaving his parents and

two younger sisters. Faced with critical decisions about his wounded acting career, Paul had recalled an earlier period of confusion about his future direction while he was an undergraduate student at the London School of Economics. He found himself working hard and succeeding academically at this prestigious university, internationally renowned for educating scholars, statesmen, and business leaders. But Paul harbored a secret desire to act. Unbeknownst to his parents, this dream was channeled into covert involvement with the theater in London. While completing his bachelor's degree, he maintained an active involvement in the University Drama Society. Paul had known he could not share his early acting accomplishments with his parents. They had literally banned him from acting in school plays as a teenager and would not have supported anything other than strict and focused academic work while at the university.

Paul's parents were both teachers. His mother taught shorthand, typing, and other office skills at a business school, while his father was a teacher at a school for troubled youth. His father did not receive a university degree because of the severe economic and social demands of the Second World War, but he did complete his training as an army officer at Sandhurst, a well-regarded officer training school. Paul realizes now that his own education at the London School of Economics was the opportunity his father never had. "In another age," Paul notes, "he would have undoubtedly gotten into a university and a quite good one. . . . During the Second World War, a lot of people missed out on the university or trade school education because of the demands of the war. . . . It was an age where, frankly, a lot of people missed out on adolescence."

The eldest son of a milkman growing up on the coast of South Wales, Paul's father was expected to be up at five each morning to help with the family's horse-drawn milk cart. While on active duty in the British army, his father served as a

40

security officer during the war crime trials in Italy, a less-publicized version of the more notorious Nuremberg trials. "He was an extremely strict disciplinarian," Paul recalls. "There were two ways of doing things: properly or not at all. That was his attitude."

Paul grew up in Taunton, the capital of Somerset County in rural southwestern England. Despite his parents' heavy emphasis on academics, they had little appreciation for the cultural arts and did not encourage Paul in his creative endeavors. Paul describes them bluntly: "Let's put it this way, there's not a single classical record in the house. They were not theater-goers. The idea of performing on the stage was something no one in the family had done. . . . The only book of poetry I was aware of in the house was a book my mother had of Rudyard Kipling's poems a generation earlier. This was a working-class Welsh family. The arts were something which were foreign to them, I'm afraid." Although journalism was considered a more acceptable career possibility in the eyes of his parents, Paul recalled that he submitted his first article for publication without telling his parents. "I sold my first piece as a freelance when I was fifteen."

Paul cannot recall how his parents reacted to this creative accomplishment at such a young age, but he clearly remembers their reaction when he openly acknowledged being gay. Paul was twenty years old when he decided it was time to talk to his parents. He had chosen to speak to his mother first. He had considered her "the path of least resistance," but her initial response proved distressing to Paul. "She couldn't understand it . . . flabbergasted. . . . No one in the family had ever been before. What had she done wrong?" Paul recalls his mother's mixed reaction of guilt and denial. "My mother would put her hand on her heart and claim (and believe it) that she didn't know a single homosexual until I told her." She was quick to protect him from his father, however, and reluctantly agreed to be the bearer of bad news.

41

To this day, Paul has never talked about his homosexuality directly with his father. "We've never really discussed it. When they were over here a while ago, I had been dating somebody for about eighteen months. The relationship was coming to an end, but I invited him and them to dinner and to the theater. I was just fed up with the fact that they didn't know. They'd never met anybody who was or had been important to me. I think what became of great ire to them is that they'd intellectually, doubtless, done the homework and come to terms with the fact that men could find men attractive and women could find women attractive. I don't think until Angus died they realized the depth of emotional contact, the depth of emotional importance gay relationships could have."

The extreme denial Paul recognizes in his parents' response to his acknowledging his homosexuality is paralleled by his own inner conflict and self-doubt as a teenager coming to terms with being gay in the 1970s. He was aware of his homosexuality as early as age twelve or thirteen. "I even knew before I had a first sexual experience. I felt extremely guilty and, to be honest, there were thoughts of suicide even then." It was a difficult period of transition, as it is for all gay teens. "I did not know why I was gay as a teenager," Paul continues. "I had a miserable adolescence. I felt I had cancer. I prayed to God for it to be removed. To me it was the most awful thing that could have happened."

Following his first brief and rather abrupt homosexual experience, Paul's self-deprecation worsened. "I felt soiled. I felt I was evil. I felt extremely lonely, very isolated, and also that it was going to ruin my life and all the dreams and hopes and everything I wanted in my life. . . . I was brought up in a community where it was most certainly wrong. It was never discussed in church, but if it had been I don't think there would have been any doubt what the teaching would have been. I was a gay adolescent who felt extremely guilty about being the person I was."

42

Paul's confused and conflicted identity, undermined by tremendous guilt and anxiety about his sexuality, continued throughout his teenage years. At the age of nineteen, his desperation led him to volunteer for a new experimental treatment called electroaversive therapy. Designed to alter his sexual orientation, the behavioral treatment promised to extinguish his homosexuality and replace it with a more acceptable brand of heterosexuality. The therapy was administered by a psychiatrist on an outpatient basis at the Institute for Psychiatry in London, also known historically as the Royal Bethlam Institute, or "Royal Bedlam," as Paul calls it. A simple and direct corrective procedure would strap electrodes to Paul's arms and legs and would shock him as he viewed slides of naked men. Viewing naked women would result in the absence of shock, supposedly reinforcing a heterosexual orientation. "It was a particularly ghastly experience to go through," Paul concludes, "and I ended up coming out of that experience knowing, realizing first of all that I was gay, which was a word at the time I still was not using, and that was to be my lot in life."

It was at this time, during the mid-seventies, as Paul recalls, that he "started drinking like a fish." His depression deepened, providing fertile ground for alcoholism to take root. By the early eighties Paul was showing the classic signs of being a full-fledged alcoholic: daily drinking, blackouts, and increasing denial and self-deception. In addition to his drug of choice, alcohol, Paul occasionally smoked marijuana and used cocaine. Looking back at his life during that period, Paul realizes that he existed in a haze much of the time. He continued to write and act when he could, but was slowly starting to realize that alcohol was adversely impacting on his health, interfering with his achievements, and destroying his relationships.

In the early eighties, Paul lived with an older man for several years, but his drinking created instability in the relationship from the start. "If I'd known about couples' counseling, if I had gotten sober . . ." Paul reflects. "It wasn't all my fault, but a significant part of the equation was my fault. There's no doubt about it." This relationship ended before Paul learned of his HIV status, before he met Angus for the first time, and before he became sober.

"The greatest achievement of my life is getting sober," Paul resolutely declares. "When I think about what my life was like before . . . you know, I have complaints about life today, but not compared with where my life was. It's changed a lot." Paul notes with certainty that deciding to become sober was a major turning point in his life. It represented a significant step away from the self-destructive and self-defeating patterns that formed the basis for his suicidal thinking. "It's never too late to become the person you might have been," Paul says, referring to a quotation by noted British author George Elliot.

In becoming the person he is, Paul attributes much of his developing emotional stability and sense of direction to his active involvement with Alcoholics Anonymous. He has been sober for more than nine years, beginning June 29, 1987. Paul has continued to attend at least one AA meeting a week ever since, acknowledging his commitment to renew his sobriety and to maintain his allegiance to the twelve-step tradition.

In keeping with the twelfth and final step, which outlines the principle of anonymity, Paul prefers to protect the identity of his first AA sponsor in London, but describes him as a well-known British actor who played a major supporting role in his journey to sobriety. He also helped Paul through the critical period when his HIV status became public knowledge. Paul remembers this man as someone who exemplified the AA tradition of "genuine humility" and understood the importance of placing moral principles above personalities. Through his wise and sustained guidance, he helped Paul to feel connected rather than isolated. "He had enormous humility," Paul reflects, "and he talked about his own personal weaknesses and problems to me. And made me feel somewhat less unique. Every alcoholic thinks he's unique. But alcoholics, when they're high, they're the worst of the worst. They beat themselves up."

For Paul, the importance of identifying with a group such as AA goes beyond the balance and stability he has achieved in his sobriety. Group identification has also allowed him to feel "less different" from others, to feel that he belongs. He has come to feel that his relationships are based more on who he is as a person than what he has accomplished or the status he has attained in his life. "AA is the only place in the world," he remarks candidly, "where a multimillionaire can be sitting next to somebody living on welfare and neither of them think there's anything in the least bit odd about it."

Even his HIV status does not serve to separate Paul from others in his group. He has been involved in a special group within AA for people living with HIV and AIDS. Issues about coping with life and facing imminent death have taken on special importance in this particular subgroup. The death of individuals within this group, in which last names are not used, has taken on special meaning, reaching beyond the formal obituaries announced in the newspapers where the person's identity is revealed.

In keeping with that tradition, Paul is certain his own obituary would not identify AA as a central part of his life. Instead, it would note that he recently retired from his position as a stock broker for a small investment bank in midtown Manhattan; that he had been prolific in his acting and writing accomplishments spanning many years; that he had been active as a deacon at the Rutgers Presbyterian Church in Uptown Manhattan; and that he had continued to compete in marathons both here in the United States and abroad until precluded by his failing health. "In my obituary, it will most certainly mention that I died of AIDS—if that is to be my cause of death," Paul says. "My friends know that I despise the cloak that some families use to conceal both the sexuality and the cause of death of their offspring. As someone who has written about HIV and AIDS regularly, why would I choose to keep my cause of death a secret?"

Paul worked as a stockbroker for just a little more than two years before retiring on disability. In accordance with his theatrical style, Paul felt compelled to arrange for his own retirement party. By design, it was planned for the eighth anniversary of his sobriety. His friends presented him with a poster filled with half-serious messages: "You're not really retiring, just moving on and on and on"; "Thank you for your friendship and guidance and for redefining retirement"; "Forget it, retirement doesn't suit you." Paul is somewhat tearful and nostalgic as he recalls the support he received from so many friends. He also reflects that this brief period with the investment bank had finally won him the approval of his parents, who had sent him off to the London School of Economics many years earlier to prepare him for an appropriate business career.

Paul is circumspect about his health, noting only that episodic fatigue was making it more difficult to maintain a regular work schedule. He did not take any prescribed medications, preferring his own regimen of vitamins coupled with plenty of exercise. Paul describes an ambitious schedule of running in Central Park about five days a week for six miles at a time. A dozen medals hang on the edge of a shelf in his apartment, attesting to his accomplishments in various races over the four short years he has been running competitively.

"I want to keep going as long as I can," Paul declares. Despite bouts of fatigue, he has continued to set prodigious goals for himself in every area of his life. His running, in particular, provides the necessary antidote to combat the helplessness and hopelessness which he sees as endemic among many of his friends with HIV and AIDS. "I would give my right arm to qualify for Boston next year," Paul exclaims with unbridled exuberance. The Boston Marathon, the "granddaddy of all marathons," is primarily limited to runners who have completed officially sanctioned races within specific time limits depending upon age groups. Paul's best time is three hours and twenty-four minutes, just nine minutes short of qualifying. But he notes that he has never really trained for any specific race, simply preferring to run as many races as he can. In 1992, he ran in more than twenty races, including four marathons and six or seven half marathons. Although Paul is aware that the Boston Marathon allows for some entries of unqualified runners through a lottery system, he is adamant that his only option is to qualify by running his fastest time ever. "I won't apply for a lottery," he states resolutely. "If I'm getting in the Boston Marathon, it's because I'm ready to race."

Paul finally told his parents about his HIV status two days before running the London Marathon in April of 1992. "I promised myself that I was going to tell them before I got back to the United States," Paul explains. "I didn't want them finding out at the end of a phone call from a doctor in New York that I was in the hospital ill. I didn't think that was fair. But also I wanted to arrange the troops. Like fighting a battle, you pick the lines you want to fight a battle on."

"Well, no one in my family has ever run a marathon before. And so the marathon was on a Sunday. I told them on a Friday. I was telling them two pieces of information. One, of course, there's concern. I mean, statistically it's going to kill me. But the other thing is, I'm in excellent shape. Apart from telling you my father was a British army sprint champion back in the forties, no one in the family had ever been as physically fit. And so, I was giving them the information but putting it in the best context I could. I mean, if I were sick I wouldn't finish the marathon."

Unlike some individuals who look upon their medical

illness as a "gift" that transforms them, Paul made it clear from the start that for him AIDS is a curse, the enemy he is committed to fight constantly with every fiber of his being. He does feel, however, that being HIV positive has been a catalyst, changing him in many ways and forcing him to actively search for a reason why he is here, to give meaning and purpose to his life. Paul has come to terms with being gay but feels the absence of a significant long-term relationship in his life thus far. "I would love to be in a successful relationship," he admits. "If I died suddenly tonight, you would say, 'He did this, he did that, he traveled, he was in a film nominated for an Oscar, he did a TV series, he wrote newspaper columns.' You'd say, 'My God, he did quite a lot. But the one thing he didn't achieve was a successful one-to-one relationship.' And in a way, it's getting more difficult."

Paul pauses to reflect for a moment, then continues: "People who are HIV positive are very frightened of getting involved in relationships because they're frightened it's not going to work. . . . Some people just want to sort of live out the rest of their time taking as few risks as possible."

Paul's risk taking includes a play he finished writing. With the right mixture of pride and humility, he declares it "some of the best writing I've ever done." Focusing on just two characters, a drag queen and a stand-up comedian, the play portrays their struggle to sustain a relationship. In discussing his writing, Paul reveals, "I tend to use it as a way of writing about things I think about or things that matter to me."

As he contemplates other areas of risk taking in his life, Paul realizes that writing is his way of redefining purpose and meaning by conveying his views on sensitive and often controversial topics. While he does not consider himself an AIDS activist, Paul is not afraid to devote his regular newspaper column on religion to confront the views of the Christian Coalition on such controversial topics as homosexuality, feminism, and abortion. In writing articles for runners' magazines about HIV-positive athletes, Paul confesses that he is "subversively" attempting to erode the public stereotypes about the impact of AIDS on athletic careers. At the same time, his personal interviews with world-class runners serve to bolster his own determination to continue competing despite the medical odds.

Paul's own busy schedule includes a tour of his play based on the life of John Keats, revived to commemorate the anniversary of his birth two hundred years ago. Paul has always been aware that his fluctuating and unpredictable energy level may prevent him from completing what he started, but his uncertain physical health has not discouraged him from pursuing his goals. "Touring is tiring," Paul explains. "It's hard work. Sleeping in strange bedrooms, catching planes at odd times to make connections, hiring cars and driving a hundred miles between dates, you know, it's going to be fun."

Paul projects an attitude of exuberance, desire, and determination as he anticipates achieving more in the life he has left to live. "It's going to be fun" was the resounding feeling as he discussed his Keats revival, a recently signed book contract, and his most recent play heading for production. Although some might argue that Paul is operating blindly under a heavy cloak of denial, he actually maintains an inherent faith, a spiritually based drive, which helps him cope with life and impending death.

"I believe very strongly and clearly in a God," Paul explains forthrightly. "I don't mean to say I don't have problems with God sometimes. There is still the question—and I never ever heard a satisfactory answer from anyone—about why horrific things happen. When Angus died I was extremely . . ." Paul pauses to quell his emotions before continuing. "Why did it have to happen to Angus? Why is this happening? Honestly, I don't know. The only thing I can say is, I cannot believe and conceive that this world could happen without the existence of a God or a higher power."

With an admitted sense of contradiction, Paul confesses to keeping a copy of *Final Exit* in his apartment. Although he acknowledges the importance of a higher power, he is prepared to face death with the same dignity and determination he values as guiding principles in his life. In contemplation of life's final chapter, Paul is candid and practical. "Without being dramatic about it, I can and could, having observed what I've observed, envisage the situation where I would wind up taking my own life, where my health gets in such a stage that I no longer want to live. I can imagine that happening. I've talked about it. I even talked to my doctor in England about it, exactly how it's done in terms of morphine and how the patient has control of the dosage and the patient's wishes are respected." Paul's light-hearted demeanor is suspended as he considers the profound complexities of assisted suicide. "Outside of that," he continues, "if somebody is not facing that situation, the obvious one is that suicide is the permanent answer to what is possibly only a temporary problem."

When friends have advised Paul to slow down and take life easier, to be more cautious of his fluctuating fatigue, his response has always been the same. He reminds them that when he dies, he'll be dead for a long time. In the meantime, he plans to live life to the fullest, to "keep going as long as I can." In line with this philosophy, Paul refers to a quotation from one of his favorite artists, Georgia O'Keefe: "I've been absolutely terrified every moment of my life, and I've never let it keep me from doing a single thing that I wanted to do."

On a bright but brisk day in November 1995, Paul and more than 30,000 other runners huddled nervously in a dense pack, trying to stay warm while facing the starting line at the foot of the formidable Verrazano Narrows Bridge in New York City. Gleaming in the morning sun, the bridge swayed with the strong wind and the weight of the runners as they made their way across the bay to the borough of Brooklyn and then over the 26-mile, 385-yard course to the finish line in Central Park. For Paul, just showing up and being part of the race was a victory in itself, for it reminded him that he had lived to face another day, yet another goal accomplished in his life.

Along with the surge of adrenaline in anticipation of this defining moment, Paul was more clear of mind and purpose than he had ever been before. In facing life, Paul could derive comfort and strength from the words of Dylan Thomas, the same poet he had chosen for his eulogy to Angus: "Do not go gentle into that good night . . . Rage, rage against the dying of the light."

The starter's pistol broke through Paul's thoughts with a sharp crack, and he felt himself propelled forward with the surging momentum of the race. The finish line was far away, but Paul could envision himself already there.

4

The Longest Race

The best runners from every country were there. The whole world was watching anxiously, waiting for the start of the race. This was the 1996 Summer Olympics, hosted by the proud and hospitable citizens of Atlanta, Georgia. A spacious new stadium had been specially constructed for the track and field venue. Under bright lights shining high in the darkening sky, the stadium was packed for the final day's events. The atmosphere was electrified with anticipation as the competitors milled around nervously at the starting line, waiting for the finals of the women's 5,000-meter race to begin.

Mary surveyed the undulating ocean of colors in the stands wrapped tightly around the island below of bright green grass edged by the reddish brown track. Focusing more closely on the spectators, Mary was struck by the complexity of sights and sounds. Faces of every shade and clothing of every hue were punctuated by a cacophony of ethnic languages.

Mary was a petite woman, her thin, somewhat drawn face framed with auburn hair cut short. Her lips were pressed tightly together with the tension of the moment. Her eyes would brighten periodically, then squeeze shut as she felt yet another wave of mixed emotion surge through her. She felt a swelling of anxiety as though she were losing touch with her familiar zone of comfort. At the same time, she felt a twinge of emptiness with each thought that she did not belong here in this mass of enthusiastic, smiling people.

Mary recognized the anxiety as her own surge of adrenaline. It was an immediate, visceral connection to the elite group of distance runners on the track down below who were jockeying for position behind the starting line. This rush of adrenaline was both the familiar friend and the dreaded foe Mary had experienced before every race she had ever run. From the age of twelve when she first joined her older brother David on the school cross country team in Wilkes-Barre, Pennsylvania, until her last official race as a freshman at Georgetown University in Washington, D.C., this adrenaline-fueled anxiety was her constant companion. She knew that other runners viewed her as a tough competitor, gifted with stamina and endurance, but Mary always felt scared that she would fail or that her best would not be good enough. She always felt guilty when she did not run to the point of complete exhaustion.

Despite her feelings of inadequacy and worthlessness, Mary proved herself to be a talented runner early in her competitive career. She remembered coming in third in her very first invitational meet, a race of 1.7 miles in Kirby Park near her family home in Wilkes-Barre. Encouraged by the high school coach and her older brother, Mary tested herself in local competitions. As a seventh grader, she gained considerable recognition as the first and only female to finish the five-mile Cherry Blossom Run. Later she would win the district championship in her first year of varsity competition.

Throughout high school, Mary persisted in her efforts to run among the best until she finally won the state cross country championship in her senior year. With her seventh-place finish in the national cross country finals in San Diego, California, Mary qualified for first team all-American. Her national prominence was further reinforced by finishing just seconds behind the world-class distance runner Joan Benoit in the L'Eggs Minimarathon held in New York City's Central Park. Before heading off to college at Georgetown University, Mary continued to prove herself with successful performances in international competition. Clearly she was on her way to becoming an accomplished world-class athlete with the potential to compete with the best, perhaps finally deserving of her Olympic dreams.

Behind the facade of the tough competitor, however, was a fragile self-image insidiously eroding the tenuous boundaries of her publicly acclaimed stamina and endurance. Growing up in the mountainous mining region of northeastern Pennsylvania, Mary felt she was a social misfit from early on. Beyond the shy awkwardness characteristic of many adolescents, Mary constantly struggled with her feelings of inadequacy and consuming self-doubt. Running became a compulsive outlet for Mary's obsessive need to prove that she belonged among the best.

Before long, Mary's weight became the focal point for measuring her success, not only as a runner but as a woman. This self-conscious preoccupation with the numbers on the bathroom scale quickly surpassed in importance her mounting collection of running medals. In a futile attempt to control her weight, Mary says that food was "an enemy waiting to devour me." Her fear of unrestrained eating was compounded by a secret desire to binge beyond satiation. By her senior year in high school, Mary was well entrenched in a severe eating disorder, an obsession with food, weight, and thinness that would consume her time, her energy, and her emotional health.

During the critical transition period of her freshman year at Georgetown University, Mary's eating disorder dominated her every waking minute. While her weight dropped precipitously, Mary continued to run competitively, striving to be the best while at the same time feeling increasingly worthless and alienated. Her preoccupation with food was compounded by a growing sense of spiritual emptiness. She felt worthless to God as well as to herself. Added to the self-absorption and social withdrawal that most victims of eating disorders adopt to hide their illnesses, Mary was having increasing difficulty with concentration, memory, organization, even basic self-care.

Alarmed and distraught, her parents encouraged Mary to seek help. An appointment was made with a psychiatrist in Washington, D.C., a specialist in eating disorders who properly diagnosed Mary as suffering from anorexia nervosa and recommended hospitalization. This was Mary's first opportunity to receive the appropriate professional help she so desperately needed. However, at the time of this important turning point, she recalls feeling a pervasive sense of hopelessness. The only way out was to die, she remembers thinking.

After three excruciating weeks in the psychiatric unit of Georgetown University Hospital, Mary was transferred to Wilkes-Barre General near her home to continue treatment. She was on antidepressant medication and had gained some weight, but she continued to feel hopeless and depressed. She viewed herself as an abject failure in her attempt to make it both as an independent college student and as a competitive runner. Mary recalls that her secret thoughts of suicide became more strident and compelling following her discharge from the hospital.

It was November 1981 when she arrived home just in time to celebrate Thanksgiving with her family. "If I learned anything during the course of my psychiatric treatment," Mary concludes, "it was that I could live life neither in the future nor in the past. I was trapped in the present with only one clear way out."

That way out proved to be more difficult to attain than Mary had anticipated, however. A massive New Year's Eve overdose with an assortment of pills succeeded only in initiating a humiliating and distressful episode of having her stomach pumped at the emergency room, followed by another period of inpatient psychiatric treatment. Looking back at her initial reaction following the suicide attempt, Mary recalls feeling happy to be alive. "For the first time in months, I was glad of it. I'd been granted a second chance at life. It wasn't too late."

During this second hospitalization, Mary found it therapeutic to write every day in a diary she called "My Journal: The Story of a Girl's Return to Life." One of her entries was a poem which expressed many of her most confusing and profound thoughts about life, connections with others, and feelings of despair and inadequacy:

> I wish I was born with more love
> For the people around me and God up above.
> They tell me I have so very much to give
> But will I be able to really live?
> To take the good and the bad and be willing to dare?
> To quest for knowledge and perfection of health?
> To work hard each day to gain some wealth?
> Moment by moment life is passing me by
> And yet I stand still unable to cry.
> Oh, life precious life, will I ever know?
> To be spurred on to tasks that can make me glow?
> I'd never give up, I was the girl with the heart.
> How did I grow so very far apart?
> A family filled with love and joy;
> Always caring was a special boy.
> But yet I'm living in a world that's cold
> Separated from all others, I'm told.

> I try and try but just can't connect—
> Living alone in my isolated world,
> I don't ask for riches or wealth or glory—
> Just a feeling of warmth
> That wouldn't leave me in a fury.

Mary's hidden fury and despair continued to deepen following her discharge from the hospital on February 2, 1982. Mary remembers the discharge summary noting her to be "no longer suicidal, not psychotic, and only mildly depressed." She remembers wishing it were true. But she knew at that time what she needed to do to end the pain, depression, and feelings of worthlessness that consumed her. She knew how, when, and where it would take place. There was no uncertainty, no ambivalence. Two days after her discharge from the hospital, at the age of eighteen, Mary was ready to end her life.

Black Diamond Bridge stood dark and ominous against the winter's night sky. The air felt crisp and cold as she carefully balanced herself on the steel beam extending out over the icy waters of the Susquehanna River below. With calm, quiet deliberation, she stepped off. Mary remembers screaming as she fell. She remembers the darkness and the numbness that quickly enveloped her. There was no splash as she expected. Instead, she found herself lying on a solid slab of ice. Her body was completely without sensation, unable to move. Before losing consciousness and unable to cry out because her lungs had collapsed on impact, Mary remembers praying in desperation: "I don't want to die, God! Please save me!"

The sharp crack of the starter's gun snapped Mary back from the memory of cold numbing darkness to the bright lights of the stadium gleaming in the summer night. The Olympic 5,000-meter race was under way. She experienced the familiar adrenaline surge as she felt herself matching the efforts of the runners rounding their first turn on the track, strategically negotiating for position while settling into their long, loping strides. Mary knew in her mind what this kind of performance demanded, but her body—more specifically, her legs—had long forgotten the routine. In place of feeling the taut muscular thighs and lean calves she had meticulously toned over many years of training, Mary now could feel only muscle spasms in her back against the confining frame of her wheelchair.

Mary's leap from the bridge more than fourteen years earlier had not taken her life, miraculously, but she was left with a fractured third thoracic vertebra in her spine. Emergency surgery was successful in fusing the vertebra, but Mary developed a blood clot and was in danger of dying before she was revived and the operation completed. Drifting in and out of consciousness for several days in the intensive care unit at Mercy Hospital, Mary remembers feeling happy to be alive. She felt closer to the family she attempted to leave behind, and was more determined than ever to live her life fully, more connected to others. "The feelings of love and gratitude that welled up inside surprised and nearly overwhelmed me," Mary reflects. "They were feelings I hadn't experienced for months—feelings I was afraid I'd lost forever."

With a respirator tube in her mouth pumping air into her fragile lungs, Mary could not speak. Soon she began to write her thoughts in an effort to communicate her feelings to those around her. The pain from her multiple fractures was excruciating but Mary was determined to persevere. Helping her through the most intense periods of doubt, depression, and desperation, Mary's parents continued to support her with their presence. They encouraged her to be optimistic. The doctors had assured them that the spinal cord was not severed and that there was a remote possibility she would walk again. Mary particularly remembers her mother's optimistic message. "Whatever happens, Mary, whatever you do, you're going to be an inspiration to others. Maybe more of an inspiration than you ever could be as a runner." With the support she received from family and friends, and after spending time alone with her thoughts, Mary began to feel that God had saved her for some purpose, that there was a plan for her life and that it was up to her to listen carefully and learn what her new lease on life was meant to be.

Her older sister Judy visited Mary frequently as she moved through the next critical months of medical transition from the ICU to a regular hospital ward. Eventually she was transferred to a rehabilitation center specializing in spinal cord injuries. Throughout this period of recovery, Judy encouraged Mary to express her feelings. They prayed together for God to come into Mary's life and direct the healing process. Judy's strong fundamentalist Christian background was influential in eliciting what Mary would later refer to as a "born again" experience. In the hospital, she felt an intense emotional awakening to the spiritual presence of God in her life. Mary describes this deepening faith as the beginning of her search for forgiveness, strength, and inspiration to endure what lay ahead. "I asked God to forgive me," Mary explains, "not only for trying to take the life he had given me, but for all the wrong I'd ever done, all the good things I'd left undone. I asked Jesus to come into my life, to live in me and through me. I asked God to fill me with his own spirit and to begin to change me into the kind of person he wanted me to be."

Through reading the Bible and prayerful meditation, Mary began to see the strengthening of her spiritual beliefs as a significant dimension of the healing process. Her renewed faith helped her to endure the pain of repeated spinal cord surgeries. Operations were followed by weeks of mind- and body-wrenching restraint in various traction apparatuses, and months of exhausting physical therapies. Mary often perceived these trying treatments as personal tests of her new-found relationship with God and as critical challenges to her commitment to live her life differently, to live her life with more strength and purpose.

Mary began to see the long road to recovery as the hardest race she had ever run. Each phase in rehabilitation brought with it an emotional roller coaster of promise and pain, exhilaration and exhaustion, hope and heartache. Mary attributed much of her emotional and physical endurance to her deepening faith, to the many friends she made along the way, and to the unwavering presence and support of her family.

Among the multitude of medical and rehabilitation personnel who attended to her, Mary recalls the encouraging conversations with Dr. Richard Fitzgibbons, a Philadelphia psychiatrist whom she talked to on the phone every few days. He encouraged her spiritual journey, taught her the therapeutic value of prayer, and helped her to differentiate among the numerous conflicting emotions that flooded her daily.

It was not until nearly two months later that Mary would finally meet Dr. Fitzgibbons in person. She was immediately struck by his silver hair and distinguished features but could not help noticing his slight build and the limp when he walked. Mary felt that Dr. Fitzgibbons understood what she was feeling, thinking, and experiencing. His compassionate caring and unconditional support would be an important anchor for her as she progressed and regressed through the many months of rehabilitation until she was finally discharged in December 1982.

Mary arrived home just in time to celebrate Christmas with her family. Reflecting on the work that lay ahead, she became painfully aware of the possibility that she might never regain the use of her legs, never walk again, never run another race. "I was forced to face my limitations and challenged to use all my strength to master the survival skills required for a lifetime as a paraplegic," she recalls.

Mary's focus now returned to the Olympic stadium surrounding her. Having completed their race, the runners were now stretching their tired limbs in an effort to cool down. Identifying with their exhaustion and pain, Mary reflected on her life as a paraplegic. Clearly, she could appreciate some of the advantages. The availability of handicapped parking spaces and the special seating provided in wheelchair-accessible places certainly were a convenience. But these few privileges could never compensate for the interminable pain and physical and emotional restriction on her independence. Parking privileges didn't make it easier to wake up each day trying to feel optimistic that life might get better and better.

Over the years, the struggle to face life as a paraplegic has taken its toll on Mary's ability to cope. Despair and self-doubt have often left her vulnerable to repeated bouts of crippling depression, which trigger many of the same suicidal thoughts and symptoms that propelled her fateful leap from the bridge. As an important part of self-therapy, Mary continues to write about the inner struggle to fight the demon depression and enduring pain. She writes about her efforts to overcome the eating disorder which continues to plague her damaged body image. She writes about discovering the meaning and purpose of her life as a paraplegic.

Most notable of her writing efforts was a book that was eventually published in 1989 under the title *Dark Marathon*. It was completed with some assistance from a professional writer. Mary's personal account of her life, her near death, and the ongoing process of physical, emotional, and spiritual recovery, became the object of much public attention. She found herself responding to a flood of letters and phone calls from people who were inspired by her story, who identified closely with what she was going through, and who simply wanted to communicate their compassion and caring.

After numerous articles about her and several nationally televised interviews, Mary eventually discovered her new identity as a role model. She found herself in a position to advise vulnerable young athletes pushing themselves to be number one, women with eating disorders striving for unobtainable perfection, and desperately depressed people facing suicidal crises in their lives. Perhaps her mother had been right when she prophesied that Mary would inspire more people as a paraplegic than she ever could have as a world-class distance runner.

Back at the Olympic Stadium in Atlanta, Mary watched the medal ceremony for the three women who had proven themselves the best in the world. She remembered how difficult it was being in the spotlight on the world stage. People the world over could celebrate your success as a winner. But if you were to lose, the agony of your defeat would be there for all the world to judge. Mary became painfully aware that the success of her book and the resulting public scrutiny of her physical and emotional recovery were partially responsible for the next in a series of significant downfalls.

The period of time covered by her book included several psychiatric admissions to stabilize her debilitating eating disorder and treat her deepening depression. In the closing chapter, Mary courageously wrote about her last suicide attempt, which followed her discharge from the eating disorders unit in a hospital near her sister's home in Virginia. Released to live in her own apartment with a roommate who assisted her, Mary viewed this as her first experience living independently from her parents since her disastrous freshman year at Georgetown many years earlier. It soon became evident, however, that this was not to be a success. Mary's depression was back, fueled by anorexic deprivation and bulimic binging. Once again she found herself contemplating suicide as the only way out of the unbearable emotional, physical, and spiritual pain.

The overdose of antidepressant medication was potentially lethal, presenting the risk of irreversible heart damage, but Mary was discovered in time. After having her stomach pumped and spending a week in the hospital, she was discharged back to her parents' home in Wilkes-Barre, just in time to spend Christmas with the family. Once again, Mary was glad to be alive but saw herself as an abject failure. Mary had hoped to conclude the last chapter of her book with strong and inspiring evidence of her successful recovery. Instead, she chose to face the sober reality that this was to be a long and difficult process, more difficult than any race she had ever run in the vital prime of her youth.

The final paragraph of *Dark Marathon* resonated prophetically for Mary: "I may even fall again. But I'm hopeful that the lessons I've already learned will enable me to scramble back up more quickly in the future. I still can't see the finish line. But that's okay, because I know now that real spiritual and emotional healing and growth is a lifelong, marathon process. And with God's help I intend to stay in this race to the very end."

Now, at the age of thirty-three, Mary can look back at the nearly eight years of her life that were not captured on the pages of her book. They were years that continued to unfold in a roller coaster ride of episodic successes and painful setbacks. In the year following her graduation from King's College in Wilkes-Barre, Mary struggled through yet another serious depression and subsequent hospitalization. Looking back at this desperate period, Mary feels that in many ways this last episode of depression was more painful than all the others. "It was worse than '82," Mary concludes, thinking back to the suicide attempt that had condemned her to a wheelchair. "I had been through all this before. Didn't I learn anything? I mean, here I'd written a book on it."

Mary realizes now that as much as the book had been an important part of the healing process, it also represented a kind of curse. Her writing contributed to the false and fragile belief that understanding and analyzing your experiences should protect you, that insight should provide a preventive against future illness. Referring to her last relapse into depression, Mary realizes that she felt a tremendous sense of guilt that she had let people down who looked up to her as a role model, guilt that she had failed those who wrote to her for encouragement and support. But most of all, Mary felt that she had disappointed God once again. "The thought that haunted me the most was that God gave me a second chance at life," Mary reflects. "God gave me everything: the best doctors, friends, family. God gave me everything and I blew it."

This last depression occurred at another critical transition point in Mary's life. Just as her initial depression worsened during her freshman year at college, this last episode was fueled by an overwhelming uncertainty commonly experienced by new college graduates. But Mary was nearly twenty-eight years old when she finally received her undergraduate degree. An adult in age, she felt overwhelmed by independent adult decisions. Propelled into adulthood, Mary found herself making many unhealthy decisions that summer and fall which would severely unbalance her emotional resources and coping abilities.

Achieving a healthy balance through moderation had always been difficult for Mary to maintain in the face of surging impulses and unbridled compulsions. That stressful graduation year found her recovering from major back surgery, struggling to function with chronic pain despite the use of massive pain killers. At the same time, she was going through withdrawal from tranquilizers. Against the advice of her parents and her therapist, Mary insisted on starting a premed curriculum, including a grueling duel with what evolved to be her twin demons—chemistry and calculus. Adding more stress to her life at the time, she was developing a relationship with a man in Boston who had shown increasing interest in her. "I felt I was very much in love with him," Mary recalls. "And I started to believe that this was going to turn into something."

Mary's impulse toward grandiose excess was physically propelling her back into a rigorous exercise regime. Running was no longer an option; wheelchair racing now became her driving passion. She joined a racing team and traveled with the team throughout the Northeast competing in wheelchair track races. Following the daily hours spent training on a track near her apartment, Mary pursued competitive swimming. This compulsive exercise regime seemed to be Mary's attempt to release the insurmountable energy that prevented her from slowing down, relaxing, concentrating, reading, sleeping, or eating properly. Along with the inevitable weight loss, Mary began to lose track of her medication, sometimes taking too much, other times taking too little.

The pressure was building. Mary's physical health, emotional balance, and daily functioning became increasingly disrupted. "I couldn't relax," Mary recalls. "It was like the summer before I went away to college. It was that element of being driven that occurs whenever I get depressed. That's how it affects me. I couldn't relax. I couldn't watch TV. I couldn't go to the movies. . . . I wasn't thinking clear. There would be racing thoughts, a lot of racing thoughts." One obsession that unceasingly drove Mary was her conviction that God was leading her life: he was directing her to take on more and more, to accomplish these grandiose feats without hesitation, without delay.

With her psychiatrist, Dr. Doyle, out of the country for most of the summer of 1992, Mary's medication was her own responsibility, with some monitoring provided by aides who came to her apartment to assist her. One day late in July, an aide found Mary difficult to wake. When she did arouse from her bed, Mary appeared disoriented and unsteady, the result of ingesting triple the prescribed dosage of antidepressant medication. Despite Mary's adamant protests that this was an accidental overdose and not an intentional suicide attempt, Dr. Doyle and her parents insisted that she have an around-the-clock, live-in aide. Furthermore, she was prohibited from driving her car. Rather than feel cared for and protected, Mary perceived this imposed suicide watch as another failure in her efforts to maintain precious independence. It had eluded her once again.

Perhaps it was this sense of crushing defeat in being unable to care for herself, this loss of independence and self-esteem. Or perhaps it was the D she received in chemistry class that semester. But Mary began to experience overwhelming guilt and apprehension that she had once again disappointed God's plan for her. Despite her compulsive efforts to connect with spiritual support anywhere she could find it—through prayer meetings, friends, constant listening to Christian radio, even phone calls to strangers at Christian counseling centers—Mary was increasingly feeling "far away from God."

Looking back at this critical period, along with other episodes of depression over the years, Mary recognizes the important role her spiritual beliefs have played in both helping and hurting her. "After my accident, I began to sense God's presence more," Mary surmises, recalling the evolution of her faith. "I began a more mature and spiritual search, and it genuinely helped me accept my disability and just coming to terms with the loss of so many things." However, when these beliefs became excessive, they spun out of balance, triggering considerable pain and spiritual anguish for Mary, and compounding her vulnerability to guilt and debilitating depression.

As her emotional and spiritual balance deteriorated and her weight continued to drop, it became clear to everyone that Mary would have to leave her apartment and return home to live with her parents. Mary remembered the small glimmer of hope she felt in successfully completing one graduate school course that fall, but she knew she was severely depressed. Her depression was accompanied by raging bulimia and thoughts of suicide. As much as Dr. Doyle wanted to keep Mary out of the hospital, it became imperative that she receive inpatient care to stabilize her rapidly failing condition. By November,

Mary was admitted to her seventh psychiatric hospital.

"I went from bad to worse in the hospital," Mary explains. Dr. Doyle recommended a female therapist. Mary resisted the change in treatment, and her response to the prescribed medication proved unsuccessful. "All I would do is binge," she recalls. "I'd skip the therapies. I got a bedsore. They didn't take good care of me physically. Their attitude at this hospital was, you know, Mary is responsible for her own life . . . suffering logical consequences even if that meant me getting little sleep, not showering, not even getting out of bed to go to the bathroom and letting me lie on a plastic covered mattress with no sheets because I didn't have the initiative to make the bed."

By February 1993, Mary's condition in the hospital had not improved appreciably. Discharge options for her were limited, but further hospitalization in a state institution clearly was under consideration. Finally, it was decided that Mary would return to live with her parents. Under close supervision, she attended a day treatment program, a part of the community mental health system in Wilkes-Barre. Mary had come full circle in her psychiatric odyssey. The day program she attended was Council House, the same program she had participated in eleven years earlier before her life-changing leap from the bridge.

This second time around in the Council House program, Mary was confronted with the stultifying stigma of mental health treatment in a way that would eventually help her to accept herself once and for all, as well as other unfortunate people who shared her emotional vulnerability. She became more enlightened and more empathic. She acknowledged her identification with a neighbor and childhood friend who had struggled with chronic schizophrenia and was in and out of state hospitals without ever seeming to get better. Through her renewed friendship with fellow patients and her deeper involvement in the Council House program, Mary learned the importance of humility and compassion.

"To me it was like a stigma," Mary reflects, "because a lot of these people had been in state mental hospitals, and to me it was like, you know, pride strikes again. I mean, that was my problem from the very beginning when I was hospitalized in Georgetown. And when I left Georgetown, I was sent to the community counseling and I felt, Oh, I'm better than these people. You know, these people are just ordinary. I was a world-class runner. I was in Georgetown. I had this feeling, I guess, of superiority or that they were the dregs. You know, you hear their stories. They were beaten by their parents or molested, and I would think, How did I end up here?"

With the humility and compassion she learned at Council House, Mary slowly began to care for herself and, most importantly, to accept herself as someone who must struggle to face life each day. With this renewed sense of self and the emerging capacity to relate to the needs of others, Mary turned her energies toward volunteer work. While attending the day treatment program, Mary volunteered to work in a shelter for homeless women in the evenings. This proved to be an important turning point for her in her fight against depression, dependency, and disability. Mary began to feel that she had something to give to others, beyond what she needed to simply take care of herself. Through the encouragement of new friends, Mary experienced once again the stirrings of unfulfilled independence. She felt ready to leave the safe, but constricting, cocoon of her parents' home, the Wilkes-Barre community where she had grown up, and the mental health system where she had again found herself. At the age of thirty, Mary felt ready to make one of her most important adult decisions.

Researching the many volunteer opportunities available throughout the country, Mary narrowed her choice to the Mennonite Voluntary Service program, which supplies volunteers to work with Habitat for Humanity in Americus, Georgia. They were willing to accept Mary with her physical disability, providing wheelchair-accessible communal housing and employing her as a volunteer preschool teacher in a day-care center. Against the cautions of her parents and her psychiatrist, Mary left her support group behind and headed for Georgia in September 1993. With considerable anxiety and self-doubt, Mary felt ready to make her mark upon the world beyond Wilkes-Barre. In the process she hoped to attain the independence and self-fulfillment that had eluded her thus far in her life.

Mary quickly immersed herself in her work, taking on additional responsibilities in the church and the community, teaching Sunday School classes and leading Girl Scouts. She found herself surrounded predominantly by young people, many of whom were making their first real attempts at developing their identities through independent living. Mary perceived herself as a novice in her own emerging independence. She realized that her age, her disability, and her experiences with adversity were barriers to relating to others, leaving her feeling somewhat isolated in the community.

"I was still struggling with depression," Mary admits in retrospect. "I had not made a dramatic transition like I had in some of the other depressions." Lacking sufficient self-confidence and being without the support of a therapist for the first time in many years, Mary continued to feel like a failure. Doubting herself and questioning her future, she nevertheless pushed herself, while going through the motions of independence and self-sufficiency in her new life.

"I didn't have anybody to talk to about my deepest feelings," Mary recalls. And then she met Lowell. An energetic, spry, verbally engaging man in his early sixties, Lowell had been involved with a number of Habitat for Humanity projects. He had been divorced after thirty-two years of marriage and the raising of his five natural children and one adopted Korean daughter. Mary describes Lowell as "young at heart," but he had suffered a heart attack several years earlier. Unlike many of the younger people with whom she lived, Mary found Lowell to possess the wisdom, experience, and sensitivity she needed. More importantly, he proved to be a good listener and a true friend. Their friendship began at a potluck church supper and deepened during long walks and conversations together.

Initially Mary was self-conscious about the age difference, insisting Lowell was just a friend. But by the spring of 1994, it was becoming clear that romantic attraction was beginning to cloud the waters of their safe, comfortable relationship. "I was slow to admit it to myself, and I couldn't really talk about it with anybody," Mary confesses, "but when we finally admitted to ourselves that there was a romantic attraction there, then it was very dramatic, very intense." With their love professed, they began dating more openly and more frequently. Soon Mary and Lowell were talking seriously about marriage.

Once again, Mary found herself facing a difficult decision around a critical turning point in her life. The normal ambivalence most people feel when contemplating a marital commitment was compounded by resistance from both sides of their families. Lowell's daughters had unresolved issues about his divorce from their mother ten years earlier. They were not accepting of his remarriage to this woman half his age. Mary's family also expressed their resistance to the marriage. Not having met Lowell at the time their plans were announced, Mary's parents were suspicious of his intentions and questioned his character, resources, and background. One of Mary's brothers, who usually remained more detached, called in an attempt to dissuade her. Consistent with her protective, maternalistic and nurturing role in Mary's life, her sister Judy was adamant in her opposition, stirring up Mary's ambivalence and self-doubt while challenging their closeness as sisters.

In reflecting back on this period of intense emotional turmoil, Mary recognizes the difficulty her family faced in letting go and allowing her to function as an independent adult who was capable of making good decisions. She recognizes how strong a role Judy had played in her life and how much her parents' lives had revolved around taking care of her. "So much of their life was me. I was the focus . . . all those years when I was sick." Mary is painfully aware that her mother's physical and emotional health problems worsened when Mary left home for Georgia.

As much as Mary desperately wanted her family's support, she was prepared to follow through on her decision. She and Lowell shared a deep love. Moreover, Mary felt she was back in balance spiritually. She felt that God still had his hand in her life. In contrast to the confusing chaos of obsessive doubts and compulsive demands that characterized other periods in her spiritual journey, Mary experienced a feeling of peace and certainty in her commitment to Lowell.

On July 27, 1994, frustrated by the delays necessitated by family pressures, Mary and Lowell were legally married by a justice of the peace in Albany, Georgia. A church wedding was held a month later in the Habitat chapel in Americus. Most of their friends from the Habitat community were there, but the absence of her family and friends from the Northeast who could not attend left a void. Increasing health problems prevented Mary's mother from traveling, but her father's support was evident: he came to give her away. Mary's wedding day started a new chapter in her lifelong search for loving commitment, independence, and a healthy balance between spiritual and emotional fulfillment. This was not the Olympic feat envisioned in her adolescent dreams, but Mary knew that her marriage was her induction into an adult world where she was capable of accomplishing more than she might ever have in a lifetime of world-class track competition.

Just as she knew she had a lot to give to Lowell and he to her, Mary was determined to channel her renewed empathy and compassion into a helping profession. Her dream was to pursue her master's degree and counseling certification which would allow her to work with children in a school setting.

Drawing upon her experiences with depression, eating disorders, and physical disability, Mary has responded openly and directly to many people who have read her book or seen her in interviews and speaking engagements. Moreover, she anticipates more writing projects in the future, directed especially toward young athletes with eating disorders. She also anticipates writing an update of the emotional healing she has experienced since the publication of her book.

Physical pain is still her constant companion, and she struggles each and every day to function in spite of its distracting presence. But Mary feels more confident and determined than ever before that she will continue helping others who, like herself, have lost their way on the road from childhood to adulthood. In a more balanced and purposeful way, she feels that God has given her a gift, a gift that is guiding her in her life as a counselor. Free of the grandiosity and compulsion that characterized her strides for achievement in the past, Mary hopes to become a licensed counselor which would allow her to practice privately in addition to her responsibilities at school.

Mary admits to feeling some uncertainty about her future goals but feels confident in taking what she refers to as small "steps of faith"— faith in God's will, but a stronger, more sustained belief in herself. "I'm not sure, but it's an unsure that isn't an anxious unsure. It's more like I don't have to worry about that right now. I learned from that last depression not to panic when the picture is unclear."

At this point in her life, Mary has learned to win races by taking small but determined steps rather than being the first one to cross the finish line. "It was my endurance that brought me victories in running," she concludes. "I see the same principle holding true for me now as I engage in other areas of my life. I have always been the tortoise, not the hare. And that's okay with me."

Mary's glory as a world-class distance runner may be

behind her. But her prospects are exceedingly bright as she sets her sights on her future, a future of giving to others and providing insight, guidance, and support to those who might find themselves standing on the bridge ready to jump. Mary's race may be completed, but her journey has just begun.

5

From Mind to Music, Sanity to Song

❖

Clarity, a sense of purpose, conflict-free determination—these were the qualities that had eluded Pam at critical periods in her life when she attempted to set her goals and work out a reasonable plan to reach them. Something always seemed to happen. An obstacle would frustrate her desire or diminish her dream. Compounding this chronic pessimism, Pam realizes she was her own worst enemy in attaining most of her goals in life.

But this particular dream was different. This time she could actually envision herself in the graduation ceremony, reaching out to receive the hallowed doctoral diploma placed in her hand. This was the degree which she had doggedly pursued through these many years of undergraduate and graduate study, field placements, and the completion of her thesis research. At the age of forty, with her internship and oral thesis defense still facing her, Pam felt certain that she could overcome whatever obstacles stood in her way.

Pam's determination was etched into the lines of her face, but these lines quickly dissolved beneath an engaging smile and a hearty laugh. Athletically compact, her short blonde hair highlighted with flecks of gold, Pam was soft-spoken but exceedingly blunt. She presented an image of strength coupled with sensitivity as she outlined her future ambitions. Her professed goal was to combine her interests in research and clinical practice, helping others to overcome obstacles in their lives while trying to understand how and why people experience psychological crises. Reaching this ambitious goal would require Pam to be persistent in maintaining her emotional balance and her sense of direction.

This journey began at a crucial point in Pam's life when she found herself ready and able to confront the past, the present, and the future—all her life experiences, all her life-changing choices as well as her failure to make decisions—all at the same time. If there would be one defining moment that shaped her life, this would be it. She vividly recalls the actual scene of this transformation, the time and place when her entire thinking and being radically changed.

Fairlawn, a quiet and friendly suburban town in northeastern New Jersey, is due north of the city of Newark, where Pam grew up after moving from her birthplace in Brooklyn, New York. It was a warm, blue-skied spring day. The soft white petals of a stunning dogwood provided a protective arch over her head as she sat on the curb reading and eating her lunch. Alone with her confusing thoughts. Alone with her distorted perceptions of herself. Alone with a multitude of questions, but without ready answers.

At the age of thirty-one, what had she accomplished? Where had she been? Where was she going? After nearly ten years of mindlessly climbing telephone poles, Pam knew one thing for certain. She knew she hated her job at the phone company and needed desperately to make a change. "The phone company was making me crazy," Pam recalls. "I couldn't stand it anymore. I felt brain-dead."

Brain dead. That was how Pam viewed her mind. Surviving high school and barely enduring the few short weeks of college, Pam never considered her mind an important personal asset. From her mother's perspective, Pam was seen as the stupid child in the family; her younger sister was deemed the gifted one, the child with the most intellectual and academic potential. "She told me I was stupid from the time I was born," Pam explains. With unabashed bitterness, reflecting years of therapy to resolve her underlying rage, she soberly describes the debilitating impact her mother had on her developing self-image. "My mother took two very important things from me: she took my mind and she took my music.

"I was very good musically," Pam recalls with more regret than boastful pride. Beginning with guitar lessons in the second grade and voice lessons later, Pam enjoyed singing and playing. Her mother was talented musically as well, having performed in local USO shows when she was younger. Pam became more accomplished through performances at school, her synagogue youth group, and several coffee houses. She anticipated continuing her musical interests in college and entertained dreams of professional training to be a cantor, a singer of liturgical solos for Jewish services.

By her senior year in high school, Pam was filling out applications for auditions and interviews with college music departments. Despite Pam's obvious talents and determined sense of direction, her mother was unsupportive of her musical aspirations during this critical period of transition. Pam

77

still believes her mother intentionally sabotaged her hopes of seriously pursuing her music. "She took my mind and she took my music," Pam repeats. Of course, Pam also recognizes that her mother sabotaged her own musical career with alcoholism.

Describing her childhood as "hideous," Pam is blunt about her family life. "My mother's an alcoholic. My parents divorced when I was seventeen. My childhood . . ." Pam hesitates before continuing. "My mother wished me dead and I managed to incorporate that into my own schema. . . . It was not a good growing up. Most of it was spent picking her up off the bathroom floor and putting her to bed." Pam describes her father simply as a "non-presence" in her life. He was a "nice guy," she explains, "and he did what he was supposed to do. He worked hard and he provided for his family. He was a truck driver and he would go to work very early in the morning and come home very late at night and sleep on the weekends." Pam's father did not share her mother's drinking problem, but was unable to compensate for her mother's destabilizing influence.

Pam is uncertain about her mother's abusing her when she was an infant, but she is very clear about her mother's chronic pattern of emotional and physical neglect. Pam recognizes that her mother's alcoholism severely compromised her ability to care for herself, let alone the needs and demands of an infant, recalling her mother's anger and the irrational expectations of role reversal that are characteristic of an abusive parent. "She wanted something to save her life," Pam concludes, "and she thought it would be me. I didn't do it. I was a baby. I was a little baby. I didn't save her life. Hence, I made her life worse."

Following her parents' divorce, her mother's drinking escalated. At the age of nineteen, Pam decided she was ready to make her own break from home. She began working for the phone company, climbing telephone poles while living on her own and supporting herself. By this time in her life, Pam's own substance abuse started to escalate. She deliberately avoided the use of alcohol, professing that she never wanted to be like her mother. Beginning at the age of twelve, Pam initiated what would become a fourteen-year history of drug abuse. Ironically, the first drug she abused was her mother's pain medication. Darvon "made it better," Pam recalls. With "downs" she could begin to tolerate her life just enough to survive from day to day. She found that with downs she could resist, for a short time at least, the powerful and persistent impulses to cut herself with razor blades.

Pam recalls that her first experience with self-mutilation occurred at the age of five when she used a piece of glass from a broken jar to carve her skin. Pam soon discovered that razor blades were quicker, cleaner, and more effective. She would hide one in the bathroom for "emergency use" when her mother's emotional outbursts and incessant criticism made the pain unbearable.

Pam seemed to know early on that her self-mutilation was a desperate response to induced feelings of powerlessness coupled with rage. It would only occur to her many years later that being successful would also serve to trigger these self-destructive episodes, reminding her that she was undeserving of accomplishments. This pattern of self-inflicted pain would become Pam's own private resource for rage-driven power and consummate control. Self-mutilation provided her refuge from the rejection and failure, uncertainty and fear that threatened to engulf her. Pam's teenage and early adult years were consumed with a desperate search for anything that could either deaden the pain or bolster the illusion of control.

Her journey of self-sabotage proceeded down any chemical path that provided immediate gratification. "I was a garbage head," Pam confesses. "Whatever I could find I would use. . . . I'm lucky I have a brain left." Ironically, her own history of drug abuse would fulfill her mother's demeaning perception of her as the "stupid child." While her mother may have begun the process of diminishing her mind, Pam had shifted into high gear the destruction of not only her brain, but her whole life.

Speed, the street name for methamphetamine, soon became Pam's drug of choice. She derived pleasure from the swift surge of adrenaline that elevated her into a new world of unrestricted pleasure, complete with a grandiose illusion of control. At the same time, she continued her use of downs, pot, psychedelics—anything available to her. Pam recalls one episode when she found a bottle of unlabeled pills in the gutter and, without hesitation, ingested them. Although no significant adverse consequences followed this particular experiment, Pam's risk taking would periodically result in emergency room visits, stomach pumping, and increasing concern among her friends that she was on a fast track toward suicide.

Pam's suicidal period coincided with the turmoil she experienced in the relationships she developed after leaving home to establish herself as an independent adult. A central part of her identity, Pam discovered, was her attraction to women. Initially, Pam found it almost too easy to be with men with whom she could be sexually active but not emotionally involved. She describes these early sexual experiences simply as one-night stands. Reflecting back on this ambivalent and aimless period, Pam concludes she was "looking for a guy who would take my mind off women." Her first sexual involvement with a woman did not occur until a friend introduced her to the world of lesbianism, complete with parties, gay bars, and literature. Gradually, Pam's ambivalence diminished. She began to feel more certain and more comfortable about who she was as a woman attracted to other women. She was ready to live her life more openly.

The way Pam's "coming out" impacted her family proved to be characteristic of her relationships with each of them. First informing her sister, she received a matter-of-fact response. "Oh, I was waiting for you to tell me that," Pam recounts her sister's reply. Her father had surmised Pam's sexual orientation when he discovered lesbian literature in her apartment. Characteristic of his non-presence in her life, Pam's father simply rejected her "choice of reading matter" without actually acknowledging her homosexual identity.

The response from Pam's mother proved to be most revealing, however. "My mother dismissed me completely," Pam notes. "She went into the synagogue and said Yiska for me, which is the Jewish prayer for the dead. Ostensibly, I was dead to her. It was very dramatic." Years later, Pam recalls, her mother rationalized that her mistreatment of Pam was caused by Pam's lesbianism in the first place, because it distorted the normal mother-daughter relationship and made it more difficult for her to love and care for her.

It would take more life-changing experiences and much more therapy for Pam to finally realize that her sexual orientation and her emotional disconnection from her mother were not cause and effect. Years later, Pam would understand that her mother's constant and demeaning criticism was a reflection of her mother's own feelings of inadequacy and not a deserving consequence of Pam's confused identity, her lack of intelligence, or her own inability to love and be loved.

These insights about herself and her relationships with family, friends, and lovers did not come easily to Pam. "Lesbian relationships are not easy," she says, recalling that her most intense suicidal episodes often coincided with periods of instability or uncertainty in her love relationships. During these periods of emotional turmoil, Pam was often consumed with profound depression, impulsive rage, and incapacitating anxiety. Overdosing with prescribed medications became her primary mode of reaching out to those she felt in danger of losing. Although many of these episodes could be considered high-risk suicide attempts, Pam minimizes them simply as "gestures." She would always call someone to rescue her, she rationalizes. Moreover, she would generally get what she needed from those who cared for her during these crises. Rather than leading to a stronger connection with loving and caring, however, the desperation reflected in Pam's cries for help always weakened the already unstable relationship further, eventually ending in the rejection and loss Pam feared most.

The suicide attempt that nearly ended her life occurred thirteen years ago during the first year of a roller coaster relationship Pam describes as "difficult at best, horrible at worst." More volatile than the six-and-a-half-year loving relationship she had just ended, Pam's emotional turmoil was compounded by her attempt to abruptly stop her constant use of speed. After four days off the drug, Pam felt she was a mess physically and emotionally.

Pam recalls the conflict with her lover that preceded the suicide attempt. "We had an argument on the phone. And I was angry. I just took the phone and started beating the wall. I went over to her house and just had a horrible, horrible argument. And as I was leaving I turned and punched some cabinets and almost knocked them off the wall. Found out later I'd broken all the glasses inside the cabinet. That kind of violence was very, very odd for me. I was always self-violent; I was never outwardly violent."

Pam left her lover's apartment consumed with rage and despair. With calculated efficiency, she directed her anguish toward ending her life once and for all. She was determined that this would not be just a gesture; there would be no chance of escape, no possibility of being rescued. Pam decided this time would not be a cry for help.

With sturdy rope she obtained from her job, Pam ominously proceeded to set her plan in motion. She carefully fashioned a noose and attached it to the door hinge, purposely doubling it to make sure it would hold her weight. Before final preparations were completed, Pam made one last phone call to an ex-lover. Concealing her anguish behind a cloak of responsible determination, Pam cancelled their dinner date and asked her to feed her cats the next day since she supposedly would be on a twenty-four hour job shift. With careful attention to detail, Pam set about her final task.

She recalls putting the noose around her throat and kneeling down. She also remembers standing up and not being able to see anything. "Everything was black and I said to myself, 'It's okay, you're dying. Kneel down again. Just kneel down. This is going to be it.' The very next thing that I remember was waking up just a mess. I mean, I had bitten through my tongue. My face was a mess where I had hit the floor."

In piecing together whatever memories remain from those desperate moments, Pam surmises that the rope attached to the door hinge must have snapped under the weight of her flailing body. Her ultimate suicide attempt had failed despite all her determination and careful planning.

Pam woke up alone, physically wrenched and frightened. A call to her ex-lover initiated an orchestrated series of critical decisions. With the insistence of a therapist whom she had been seeing previously, Pam admitted herself into a private psychiatric hospital. Initially placed in a twenty-eight-day rehabilitation program for substance abusers, Pam was soon transferred to a psychiatric unit when the staff learned the details of her suicide attempt. Two months later, Pam was discharged. Still struggling with self-destructive impulses, she began buying razor blades again and hiding them around the house. They were a necessary part of her self-mutilation ritual. After eleven weeks of fighting her urges and openly revealing her suicidal thoughts to her therapist and her friends, Pam was readmitted to the hospital.

This hospitalization proved to be more effective in getting Pam moving in a positive direction. She felt better prepared to combat her overwhelming anxiety and depression, to control her destructive urges, and to confront her substance abuse.

Much of her symptomatic improvement was attributed to a new medication, one which is generally prescribed for patients with diagnosed seizure disorders. Pam's positive response to medication allowed her to feel free—perhaps for the first time in her life—from her compulsion to mutilate herself. "I never knew that life could be like this," Pam says, reflecting on her own futile search over so many years for the right drug to quiet her internal storm. She continues on this medication to this day. An antidepressant was added when the self-mutilation returned just as she was beginning graduate school. Once again, Pam was faced with the increase in anxiety and depression that accompanied success.

In addition to the medication begun during her second hospitalization, Pam also became more serious about dealing with her substance abuse. In her struggle to stay clean and sober, she began attending Alcoholics Anonymous on a regular basis, first in the hospital and continuing after she was discharged.

"Part of my discharge plan was that I had to be with people," Pam explains. "They didn't care how or who, but I could not stay isolated." AA provided the interpersonal contact she needed, and gradually she discovered the emotional support available to her at meetings. Although she tried some programs which were exclusively for gays, Pam found that "straight" meetings were more helpful to her in confronting the dynamics of her substance abuse. "The difference," she explains, "is that it's more about sobriety and less ragging about your recent affairs. It's less social. I mean, maybe for heterosexuals it's social, but for me it was about sobriety. And so I did meetings probably seven or eight a week for about four years and now I just do meetings periodically."

Pam is now anticipating the celebration of her thirteenth year of sobriety. She is very clear about the impact of her involvement with the various twelve-step programs over the years. "If you want to know what's brought me from putting ropes around my door hinge to now, it's the program. I spent a number of years getting sober, learning how to live. Working the Adult Children of Alcoholics program diligently in addition to Alcoholics Anonymous. You know, just trying to undo what had been done and just learning how to live a normal life. I spent some very, very productive years in therapy after getting clean, and through the program I sponsored people. I've always been somebody that people like to talk to."

As much as the twelve-step programs and medication were vital to Pam's long-term recovery, she also notes the role of her individual therapy, especially her relationship with her therapist. Individual therapy has not only provided an anchor and a lifeline during the emotional storms that threatened to sink her, it has also helped Pam find her own educational and career bearings as a therapist.

Reflecting back to that warm spring day sitting under the dogwood tree outside the phone company, Pam recalls her struggle to rediscover her mind—the mind that had been demeaned by her mother, devastated by her drug abuse, and devoted more toward her destruction than her well-being. What would happen if I took my mind back? Pam remembers asking herself. "When I was sitting looking at that tree, I realized that I didn't fit in anywhere. And that was hard for me. I'd never fit in, but, you know, I had friends. I thought differently than other people and I never knew what I wanted. And I said to myself, Where do you fit in? Where are you most comfortable? And it was with therapists . . . because that's the way I think. That's the way I've always thought. And I said, Well if that's where you fit in, then that's what you should do."

Pam acknowledges the critical role her therapist played, a psychologist she refers to as Nicki. Pam met Nicki while she and her lover were going to couples' counseling. The relationship eventually dissolved and her lover left therapy, but Pam continued to work with Nicki on an individual basis. Along with the psychiatrist who prescribed and monitored her medication, Nicki was an integral part of Pam's healing journey, providing an important impetus to her search for self-discovery. A gay therapist and recovering addict, Nicki was an "incredibly dynamic" woman who was candid about her own identity struggles, Pam says. By disclosing herself, Nicki was able to form a nurturing bond with Pam, a bond that became her source of stability when she was most fragile and confused. "She got in there with me and used whatever technique would work," Pam explains. "She was not withholding; she answered my questions. She treated me in a way that enabled me to develop the ego I didn't have. She was willing to merge with me without fear of losing herself."

Nicki turned out to be a significant source of support for Pam at many critical points in her recovery, but the final separation from her as a therapist proved difficult. Nicki was going through an emotional period of transition herself, questioning and confronting her own homosexuality. Pam felt abandoned as Nicki became increasingly inaccessible and emotionally unstable during their sessions. But Pam's fears and anger, characteristic of her own separation conflicts, were tempered by the empathy and compassion for Nicki that had developed over their many years of successful therapy together.

At this point, Pam knew she was healthier in many respects than her therapist. She felt ready to end therapy and move on. In her customary role of support, Nicki told Pam that she was making the right decision. Looking back on this separation, Pam acknowledges that, on the one hand, Nicki probably should have suspended her therapy caseload while she was going through her own personal struggles. On the other, Pam knew she needed to make this critical separation part of her own growth as a self-sufficient, functional person. Over the years, Pam has continued to identify Nicki as a good therapist, someone who helped her develop her own professional capacities. "She lives inside of me," Pam says. "I mean, a lot of the techniques that I bring to therapy are things that I learned from her."

Part of Nicki's legacy can be seen in Pam's developing interest and close involvement in helping people who are living with and dying from AIDS. As an "AIDS buddy," Pam listens to their fear, anger, and grief while attending to their desperate need for companionship at a time in their lives when they often feel abandoned. It has been an emotionally draining, gut-wrenching experience for Pam. "AIDS is just very much a part of me, very much a part of my life," she explains, remembering all the close friends she has lost to AIDS over the years. She has witnessed the final hours of more than fifty people who have died of this dreaded disease. They were all hard deaths, but perhaps the hardest of all was the recent death of Philip.

Four years younger than Pam, Philip was diagnosed with HIV in 1990. They first met during the AA meetings they attended back in the eighties. Both began their sobriety at approximately the same period of time and shared many of the same friends in the gay community. Both had attempted suicide when life seemed to "bottom out" amidst wild mood swings, uncontrolled substance abuse, and significant relationship breaks. Pam and Philip shared a lot in common. Their parallel outlooks on living life and facing death allowed them to develop a strong and special relationship that weathered many storms.

Philip's disease progressed rapidly. In his desperate effort to stave off the inevitable, he grasped for every new clinical drug trial or experimental procedure he could. Pam was there as a friend but often felt she was substituting for the family that had abandoned Philip emotionally.

It was exceedingly hard for Pam to watch her friend die. Not just because of the horrific physical deterioration, but because of her own emotional frustration in trying to support Philip's struggle to stay alive in the face of insurmountable odds. He did not want to let go. He would not give up the fight. It pained Pam to watch Philip, to wait patiently by his bedside while he desperately clung to what little life he had left.

"Oh God, I wish he would die!" Pam remembers praying as she struggled to be there for her friend in the last few months of his ebbing life. "I will miss him terribly. It will break my heart. But he's not happy this way." He doesn't feel well, but this is the course that he's chosen and I support him in it. I work very hard to support him. He's looking for quantity rather than quality of life. . . . He just wants more time. He doesn't want to die."

No matter how much she tried to support him, Pam knew that Philip was angry at her for not being there enough, not doing enough, just as his mother had never been there for him before her own death. "I know that there were many ways I reminded him of his mother," Pam observes, recognizing that this close identification had been part of what drew them together.

For Pam, talking about Philip's dying triggers thoughts about the controversy surrounding the issue of assisted suicide. It also stirs up feelings about surviving her own suicide attempt more than thirteen years earlier. Pam knows that as a therapist she will be working with suicidal patients. "I've had to really search my soul about what I would do as a clinician," Pam explains with some hesitation. "And what I've come to decide at this point is that if someone says to me they're going to kill themselves, I will do everything in my power to stop them. Because I believe that if you say it to me, then you want me to stop you. You're trying to reach out for help. It's the only ethical conclusion I can come to."

This ethical conclusion is not based on a belief that suicide itself is wrong, however. "Sometimes life is just too hard and too painful, and it's reasonable to put an end to that," she explains. In fact, Pam still cannot say she is glad she survived her suicide attempt. It continues to represent failure in her life. "When I woke up from hanging myself," she recalls, "I knew I would never try to kill myself again. I could not face it, that the suicide attempt didn't work. It was such a sense of failure, such a sense of total failure."

Pam has resigned herself to the prospects of living, but freely acknowledges that suicidal thoughts continue to emerge as she forges ahead, trying to find new meaning and purpose in her life. "I just have to do what I'm supposed to do and that's why I've gone from climbing telephone poles to pursuing my doctorate. As long as the doors keep opening, I'll keep going through them."

As clear as she is in her choice not to kill herself, she is equally clear in her conviction about assisted suicide. She would not assist someone else in killing themselves, even if that someone were a close friend facing imminent death from AIDS. "It's ultimately murder," she explains. "If I were to have helped Philip, I still would have known that I was murdering him. As much as I am murdering myself if I kill myself. If I were going to assist Philip, I would have had to be willing to know what could happen as a result and be clear in my conscience about that. If somebody says to me that they have been in pain for so many years, I would try to get them to a point where they could do whatever they need to do, get them to a point where they are clear enough to be able to make a decision. But it's my position to be neutral in actually helping them to kill themselves."

It was difficult for Pam to maintain this position of neutrality as she and a group of other caregivers assisted Philip over the last summer of his life. With his death in September 1995, Pam finally felt the emotional release she had anticipated for so many long, hard months. Philip had tried to make it easier for everyone by writing his own memorial service, complete with his favorite hymns—Pachabel's *Canon,* and a song by the Flirtations. But it was still hard for Pam as she struggled to say good-bye, to eulogize the life of a friend whose dying had been so intimately painful to her.

It was particularly difficult at this point in Pam's life. At the same time she was grieving Philip's death, she was also anticipating her wedding day planned for October. Throughout his last summer, Philip had talked about being there for Pam's special day. He felt particularly honored to be participating as a Chuppah holder, one of four bearers of the canopy which is extended over the couple throughout a traditional Jewish wedding ceremony. Pam, too, wished that Philip could be there as an important part of her wedding day, but she knew in her heart that he would not live that long.

The wedding ceremony and reception were held in the home of a friend. Pam and Sarah were deliberate in their invitations. As Pam noted, "I want the people at the wedding to be people who can joyously celebrate our marriage and our union, not people that I have to be concerned with in any way." That concern extended primarily to her parents, who she felt were continuing to question not only her being gay but her choice to celebrate her love for Sarah in a traditional Jewish wedding ceremony. So, her parents were not invited, but her sister and her sister's husband attended, along with Sarah's many other friends identified as "family." It was a joyous occasion, a celebration of healing and commitment for both Pam and Sarah.

Sarah and Pam initially met through a mutual friend at a Rosh Hoshana service held at the gay synagogue they both attended in New York. "It's a message from God when people meet during the High Holy Days," Pam explains. It was especially important that Sarah was Jewish, given that Pam's religious beliefs are a central aspect of her life. Pam attends synagogue regularly and maintains a kosher house, abiding by the practices and traditions of her faith.

"I always believed in God," Pam explains. "It became somewhat perverted in my earlier years as a way for me to beat myself constantly, feeling that I wasn't worthy. It became a way of dealing with the anger I felt toward my mother. I just turned it onto myself. And certainly when I hanged myself, I remember when I woke up just saying, 'I give up. That's it. I'll do whatever you want me to do.'" Her relationship with Sarah became an extension of this spiritual connection, Pam says. Their wedding was "a celebration to God for the joy of having a union like this, of such love" for one another.

"Sarah is a wonderful woman," Pam continues. "She is committed and passionate. She is ethical. She has values that are similar to mine. She's harder on herself than I am now. . . . But Sarah believes in me. She believes in people. And she's willing to really work on the relationship. Sarah and I were having a discussion last week about a difficult issue, and she looked at me and said, 'Do you think we need help with this?' I was bowled over that she would be willing to put that out there. And it meant a lot to me."

Geographical distance has complicated their relationship for the past three and a half years. While Pam has been busy completing her doctoral studies in New York, Sarah has maintained her position as an assistant director of a library in Virginia. In addition, Sarah has been busy with many writing projects, completing several ambitious works on the subject of AIDS. Both Sarah and Pam are heavily invested in working with AIDS patients. And both continue to attend AA meetings together. Sarah will soon celebrate her sixth year of sobriety.

To counterbalance the separateness of their high energy and pressured lives, Pam and Sarah have been learning to play together. Traveling back and forth between New York and Virginia, they make a point of using their leisure time to stay connected. In addition to regular workouts at the gym, Pam has introduced Sarah to snorkeling, a sport she has avidly pursued throughout her years of sobriety. Spending time together in secluded Caribbean reefs has proven to be the perfect elixir, a therapeutic panacea for all that is not right in their world. Snorkeling provides an escape from their busy lives of work and study, a means of reconnecting with each other after too much time apart, a way of staying in touch with the beauty of the world around them when the specter of AIDS and death becomes too overwhelming, a soothing balm for troubled minds and a physical release of pent-up tension, and a unique way of celebrating their union of shared love and caring for each other.

For Pam, being engulfed in the warm, crystal clear water brings her back to her inner self, her only connection to the world above a small tube that carries her exhaled breath and delivers fresh air. Floating quietly, effortlessly above a coral reef teaming with colorful life, snorkeling represents the ultimate therapy in her search for sanity. "It's perfect," Pam says. "There's nothing except this absolute world of energies, and all I hear is the sound of my own voice. My own breath. My own breathing. And it's just this myriad of images and there's nothing else."

In this serene and soundless world, Pam continues to search for the beauty of her own music, the music that has eluded her for so many years. While she has not yet begun to sing or play as she once did as a child long ago, Pam has found a silent harmonious song in the inner reaches of her mind. Soul-searching questions about worth and the meaning of life remain unanswered, but the sound of her breathing reminds Pam that she is more fully alive than she has ever been before. Living in the moment now seems more bearable for Pam. Perhaps one day she will be able to sing her song for the world to hear.

6

Between Terror and Rage

❖❖❖

As the small Cessna leveled off at three thousand feet, the jumpmaster gave a hand signal to the small group of novice skydivers nervously huddled close to the door of the plane. They readied themselves for what would come next, the ultimate test. Over the drone of the engine, the wind screaming by the open door, each of them struggled silently with their own terror.

Frank, a middle-aged man with a receding hairline and ruddy complexion, frantically searched his racing mind for the answer to one nagging question: "What the hell am I doing up here?" Before he could formulate a rational, reassuring response, he suddenly found himself standing on a small platform outside the fuselage of the plane. The wind whipped his helmet and jumpsuit, his sweaty hands tightly gripped the

93

struts under the wing. His training, brief and basic as it was, commanded him to let go; his paralyzing fear pleaded with him to hold on for dear life.

Within seconds of letting go, the plane quickly became a small white speck in the gray blue sky. The wind currents colluded with the force of gravity to propel Frank's arched body outward and downward at 160 miles an hour. The adrenaline rush he had felt when he let go was now more intense, his heart wrenching as he waited for his main chute to release. He may have even blacked out for a moment.

When the chute finally popped open, his body was yanked violently upward before settling into a slow spiral downward. Drifting with the wind, the reassuring tug of the canopy quieted Frank's pounding heart, calmed his racing mind. His breathing became deeper and more even. He experienced an exhilarating sense of peace. For the moment, it seemed like his mind was more fully connected to his body. Frank's inner terror, the familiar fear that had plagued him most of his life, seemed distant. He gently floated above the checkered farmland, at first just a pastel haze but now quickly coming into sharp focus. As the ground rushed up to meet him, he suddenly found himself rolling in the deep grass, his chute gently collapsing behind him. He felt safe. He was still alive.

Seven years later, Frank knows that the question he asked himself while awaiting that jump would take time to answer adequately. Now, at the age of forty-nine, Frank can reflect on the intellectual insights and emotional connections that have served as therapeutic guides to exploring his past, coping with his present, and contemplating his future. He now knows that his willingness to take a risk, to skydive for the first time in his life, was intimately connected with the need to confront the terror that has lived within him from early childhood on. Frank identifies this inner terror with the "accident" he witnessed as a five-year-old, when his father fell to his death.

"He did it from the scaffolding," Frank explains matter-of-factly. "It was Christmas, and he went down to the Downtown Athletic Club [in Manhattan] where he was working as a maintenance man. He was on a high scaffolding taking down lights and stuff on the ceiling." Frank's father had a helper who was down below steadying the wheels of the scaffolding which were chocked to keep it stationary.

As a child, Frank often accompanied his father to work. He remembered the helper cautioning his father while he left his position for a moment to move some chairs. Frank remembered his father leaning out over the edge of the platform, pushing against the railing, and stretching out for something that was just beyond his reach. With the unbalanced weight, the scaffolding suddenly tipped over and his father fell thirty feet to the hardwood floor below.

"It felt like my whole world had just exploded," Frank recalls, visualizing once again his father lying on the gymnasium floor, his head split open. "I was in the gymnasium by myself with him for a period of time when his helper ran away," Frank continues. "That was a really scary time because that was it; I mean, there was no one. I was by myself. I saw the blood coming out of his head. I don't know what I tried to do then, except thinking about how to get the blood back in his head. I stopped crying, and I remember telling him, 'I won't cry now if you just get back up.'"

The police soon arrived, summoned by his father's helper. Frank vaguely remembers blacking out several times while he stood close to his father's lifeless body. He tried desperately to understand how this could have happened, while he struggled to quell the mounting terror that welled up inside.

The authorities pronounced his father's death an accident, qualifying the family for workman's compensation payments. But Frank continued to struggle for years trying to understand how his father, an intelligent and agile man, would have allowed such an accident to occur. "All my life as a child, I used to say 'the accident.' And every time I said it, I would panic inside," Frank recalls, pausing to collect himself before completing his thought. "I finally realized what I saw was not a ladder tipping over. Instead, it was a man pushing against the perimeter, putting his weight against it. And he forced it. It was a stupid move. . . . I watched him work tons of times. I would never question him. But this one time in particular, what he was doing was so outrageous!"

It would be many years later—only after Frank began to understand his own "outrageous acts"—that he would finally accept his father's "accident" as just one part of a family pattern of self-destruction. Perhaps his father's tragic and traumatic death was not a suicide in the true sense of the word; nevertheless, it served to deepen the family secret, a legacy of loss which consumed Frank with terror and rage throughout his life.

In exploring the depths of his childhood terror, Frank realized that his jump from the Cessna was an unconscious attempt to experience and control the panic that engulfed the five-year-old child who had helplessly watched with horror as his father dropped from the ceiling before his eyes. Following his successful skydiving experience, Frank made a point of returning to the gymnasium where he relived his father's death inside that cavernous expanse. Now an adult, Frank felt the childhood terror less intensely. "The building had gotten smaller," he recalls. "The overpowering sense of doom left me."

Working through the confusing array of fears that consumed him after his father's ambiguous death, Frank has developed an impression of his father as a man with an intriguing past, someone he would have liked to know better. He was told that his father was athletic, a semiprofessional boxer in his prime. He earned a living as a salesman, working for the railroad, and as a maintenance man. By talking with family members, Frank pieced together an image of his father as "a high gear religious addict," a practicing Roman Catholic whose "life was dominated by Christ and the Crucifixion. Like an alcoholic needs his alcohol, my father needed Jesus on the Cross," Frank observes sardonically.

Although Frank does not have proof that his father was an alcoholic, he thinks it may have been another of the family secrets. Ironically, Frank may have inadvertently uncovered the truth about his father's drinking when, in the course of conducting research on alcoholism, he happened upon a series of photographs in *Fortune* magazine by Margaret Bourke White. These photographs depicted the inside of one of the speakeasies, which were prominent during prohibition in the thirties. One picture in particular caught Frank's eye. There at the bar was his father. "Young, serious, dapper. He was a good-looking man," Frank describes his father in the picture. "And what's classic about it is that there's a beautiful woman on one side of him at the bar, and there's a friendly-looking guy on his other side at the bar, and my father is looking directly into his martini glass which is in front of him. And the way he's looking is the way I felt so many times at the bar myself. You're looking inward. You're not even conscious of being there half the time."

While Frank has no memory of his father arriving home drunk, he recalls his mother's chronic alcoholism vividly. It was delicately referred to as her "sickness." A specific vocabulary of ambiguous terms is another legacy of family secrets. "When I was growing up we slept near one another, " Frank explains. "And if she was in an alcoholic stupor, I was terrified of her dying. So I would wake up all night, and I would listen to her breathing so I would know that she was still alive."

One night his mother fell out of bed and lay motionless on the floor. Frank was five years old at the time. This event occurred not long after his father's death. "I thought she was dead, too, " Frank recalls. "I mean, it was total panic. I ran

97

downstairs . . . got my landlady up. It was the only time I broke the silence about her drinking. It was taboo. It didn't exist, because she was 'sick,' but she was never drunk. And that was the one time that I shared my experience with someone outside, including my brother. We never talked about it with him. I never talked about it with her."

Frank was the youngest in the family but served as the primary caretaker for his mother during his early childhood and teenage years. In their relationship, Frank was physically protective of his mother. He merged emotionally with her. "She was my only living parent, so she was that link that kept me alive. I was very bound . . . Emotionally, I was bound to her."

Frank was told that he had a sister named Gracie who died as an infant seven years before he was born. He knew very little about her except that she was named after his father's favorite aunt and that she was laid out in a tiny coffin in the dining room of their flat, a block of ice set underneath to keep the body cool. Gracie's death was not considered one of the family secrets, but Frank learned early on not to ask too many questions.

Fifteen years his senior, Patrick was the older brother Frank looked to for the guidance and support he could not get from his mother. But Patrick had his own demons to fight. Patrick's alcoholism fueled the violent physical aggression he frequently directed toward Frank, who remembers drunken and violent fights that often resulted in bruises, dislocated joints, and broken bones. One episode that stands out particularly: when his brother strangled him in a drunken attempt to sexually molest him.

Although he remembers hating alcohol as a young child, Frank traces his own chronic alcoholism back to his first drink at the age of eight. He has vivid memories of his mother getting drunk at home after his father's funeral, and he remembers taking the whisky bottle away from her and pouring it down the sink. "Three years later I was drinking alcohol," he confesses. The family curse was just too powerful. Frank was drinking regularly, often daily, at the age of twelve. By the age of twenty-five, he was showing classic signs of advanced alcoholism, including hallucinations, episodic seizures, blackouts, and tremors. The warning signs were prominent, but Frank ignored them. Alcohol would consume his mind and his body, just as it had done with his mother.

He has vague recollections of terrifying his aunt and uncle one night while living in their home on Staten Island. "I thought I was in World War II," Frank confesses. "I kicked in their bedroom door about two in the morning. I thought they were the enemy. I could have killed them easily. I ended up in a bar miles from their home. And I was thrown out of the worst bar on Staten Island. They threw me out!"

It is difficult for Frank to dredge up memories of his alcoholic years and the mounting episodes of degradation and denial. Despite the clear evidence that alcohol was slowly killing him, he continued to resist the need for treatment. He was not yet ready to admit that his life was out of control. Frank felt he had not yet hit bottom, until his mother died.

The year was 1968. Frank was discharged from the navy reserves, fortunate not to have faced duty in Vietnam. Alcohol had taken its toll on his mother's health over the years. In addition, she suffered a series of strokes which left her incapacitated. Frank cared for her at his Aunt Terry's home on Staten Island until the final stroke that left her hospitalized and in a coma.

Frank recalls being at his mother's bedside. She remained comatose, near death, but was still hanging on to what little life was left within her. "She couldn't speak; she couldn't see; she couldn't move. But she could hear. I told her to die," Frank remembers tearfully. "She was in a coma, but I had gotten to the point where I said, 'Why don't you die?' I guess I gave her a very rude permission that it would be okay. 'Mom, let it go.' That was about it."

After nine days in a coma, his mother finally let go. Until the autopsy was performed, no one knew about the insidious cancer that had riddled her brain. Frank was finally relieved of his emotional bonds of responsibility for his mother. She was the last remaining parental link that kept him alive.

Within months of his mother's death, Frank overdosed on tranquilizers washed down with alcohol. To speed up the process, he cut open his wrist. "This was not a cry for help," Frank insists. "This was a passage I was going through. My life was getting very narrow. My judgments all depended on what was at the end of the tunnel I was in. And I came to a conclusion that it would be better to be dead than anywhere else. And when that conclusion was made, everything got peaceful. You know, at least I had decided to do something.

"I woke up the next morning and I was soaking in blood. But I was still there, still alive," Frank continues. He was persuaded to admit himself into a psychiatric hospital but did not stay very long. The heavy drinking continued, and within a year Frank made his second suicide attempt. "The second one was 1969," Frank recalls. "It was a drunken episode in a very hot car. I aimed it at a telephone pole, and I just hit the gas and went straight into it. I don't recall the actual concussion, but I got blown out of the car and was saved. I was right in front of a doctor's house. Incredible! I mean, he was living right there when it happened. He was out there in a minute . . . and he kept me out of shock."

After being treated and released from the hospital, Frank was already drinking heavily the same night. His drinking continued throughout his marriage. He met Rose while both were working for a Manhattan accounting firm. They were married in a June wedding in 1976. "We had good times together," Frank reminisces. "The first couple of years were great. They were really great. Honeymoon in Ireland. We could enjoy ourselves together. But it was the alcohol that took my life over completely. . . . I was lubricated all the time."

By 1985, alcohol had devastated the fragile marriage. Frank drank continuously. Rose was also falling apart physically and emotionally, overeating and becoming depressed herself. This proved to be a fateful year, Frank recalls. If there could ever be a true bottom for an alcoholic, this year was it. Frank lost his marriage, his home, his job, his brother, and very nearly his own life as the result of his third suicide attempt. Frank's recall of the chronological sequence of events is quite hazy, perhaps caused by advanced alcoholism, perhaps by emotional turmoil. Rose's depression had deepened and Frank's own drinking had intensified, so much so that the marriage finally reached its breaking point. Through her own therapy, Rose had gained the strength to throw Frank out of the house, beginning the process that would eventually lead to legal separation and then divorce.

The same year, 1985, saw the suicide of Frank's brother, Patrick. His death was disguised by the story of a heart attack, a story that seemed believable at the time, in view of Patrick's history of bypass surgery. But Frank suspected his brother's death was more than the natural progression of insidious disease.

Suicide was confirmed a year later in a letter from one of Patrick's sons who was in the house the day Patrick shot himself in the head with a .38 caliber handgun. His violent death served as a climax to the rage that had fueled his life, rage which was directed outward until heart disease robbed him of his vitality. Frank recounts his final conversation with his brother: "The last time I talked with him was when he was getting ready to go in the hospital for the operation. And he told me then, 'I feel like I'm in a gray zone.' And I didn't know what he was talking about at the time. So I told him, 'Patrick, I love you.' He said, 'yeah,' and he hung up. And that was the last time I talked with him. He couldn't say I love you. That was it. He couldn't say it."

With his brother's death, the dissolution of his marriage, and his life in shambles, Frank found himself entering his own "gray zone," a "tunnel where there's no definite statement about anything," he explains. "Whether life sucks or life is great, you're right in the middle. Your indifference colors it gray. You're really becoming very indifferent to life if you're going to kill yourself. It's not that you hate life as much as you become indifferent to it."

This gray zone of apathy and indifference, an emotional legacy of loss, left him feeling empty and worthless. Although he was attempting to reach out for help with his drinking, he could not shake his preoccupation with death. After carefully researching the toxicity of the antidepressants he had been prescribed, Frank ingested the entire bottle one night. Washing it down with a half quart of vodka, he waited for what seemed like hours for the expected peaceful shroud of death to envelop him.

What he got instead was excruciating pain in his muscles and joints followed by a violent grand mal seizure that knocked him out. Frank was rushed to the emergency room and treated for an adverse medication reaction. No one suspected a suicidal overdose. Maintaining the family tradition of secrecy, Frank did not inform anyone of his suicide attempt. "They had no idea, and I wasn't about to tell them," he says. "They let me go in a couple of days. After I hit the streets, I had a bottle within an hour. . . . I needed a drink."

This third and last suicide attempt was not the final dramatic act in Frank's alcoholic odyssey. It would take many more months of heavy drinking, blackouts, and further deterioration of his health before he reached the point of no return. In retrospect, Frank realizes that his sobriety in August 1986 was the end result of a series of small but significant self-confrontations. At the age of forty, with his life dangerously out of control, he was forced to face who he had become and where he was going.

The fear and concern he saw in his Aunt Terry's eyes forced Frank to acknowledge his own terror. Intertwined with the terror was a tremendous rage that was driving him away from the few people who still cared about him. This startling revelation was reinforced by serendipity one day when Frank happened to see himself on a TV monitor hooked to a camera in a video store. "I saw a man who was very old and near death," Frank recalls his black and white image starkly facing him. "You know, a very ugly person. Very ugly person. It made me look at me. I had to start questioning who I really was. Something had to stop me from drinking."

Frank signed himself into an alcohol rehabilitation program at Beth Israel Hospital in Manhattan. He began to work the program in earnest. He acknowledged his alcoholism for the first time in his life, and he began to deal directly with the issues that surrounded his alcoholism. One of the most critical of these issues was the family secrecy about his mother's drinking, the collusion of denial that prevented anyone from talking openly about her drinking. In a dramatic encounter with his therapist, Frank was able to openly explore the extent of his mother's alcoholism and plumb the depths of his emotional experiences as the child of an alcoholic. Frank was finally able to confront himself.

Through facing his own alcoholism and drug abuse, Frank was able to see the connection between his substance abuse and his suicide attempt. "The thought came to me and I really believed this was true: drinking and killing myself were exactly the same thing. When I picked up a bottle, that was the beginning of the suicide. So I started working on not drinking. And in doing so I was starting to work on not killing myself. Literally, I was doing suicide prevention while I was working to stop my own drinking. It became one thing. Like a fusion, two things became one. I began to work on staying alive."

Following his discharge from the rehabilitation program, Frank continued to work hard on staying alive, developing insights and integrating the emotional connections that would become major landmarks along his journey of recovery. These insights served to remind him where he had been in the past, how he had gotten to where he was in the present, and, most importantly, where he was going in the future. Frank understood that relapse was expected, but he had the support of therapists, sponsors, and the twelve-step tradition of AA to guide him back to the path of recovery.

Looking back on the first few years in his recovery, Frank recognizes that without alcohol he did not know how to open up to people. He was terrified about taking interpersonal risks. Frank had to learn for the first time how to share parts of himself in such a way that a genuine relationship could develop and be sustained.

Frank met Mary at an Adult Children of Alcoholics (ACoA) meeting where together they struggled to understand the disjointed pieces of their similar pasts. Mary was unique in Frank's eyes, unlike any woman he had ever met before. Because he was in the process of forging a healthier relationship with his ex-wife, Frank felt he was ready to risk connecting with a woman again.

"I fell in love with this woman," Frank confesses. "I really did . . . head over heels." Mary was renting rooms in her spacious Victorian house on Staten Island and soon—too quickly, perhaps—Frank moved in. "I took a chance . . . and we were friends," he says. Both had much unfinished work to do in their separate programs, and both were emotionally vulnerable at this stage in their lives. In addition to sharing a history of parental alcoholism, both Frank and Mary were codependent and had an addiction to sex. Their relationship was doomed from the start.

Despite Frank's efforts to be more open and loving, his relationship with Mary never progressed beyond a friendship. But their friendship became deeper and more permanent as Frank confronted his self-defeating, self-destructive patterns.

Frank wanted a romantic relationship with Mary, but when she continued to date other men he felt threatened, which stirred up deep-seated fears of loss, abandonment, and inadequacy, and triggered a jealous rage. "I felt myself shrinking," he explains. "I physically felt myself getting very small. . . . The pain was incredible."

Like a small child—scared, hurt, and angry—Frank found himself reverting back to an earlier pattern of self-abuse, a pattern that had served as a refuge from the emotional chaos of his childhood. Beginning at the age of seven, Frank had poured boiling water over his body to burn away the emotional pain he had not yet learned how to control. By his teen years, he had progressed to cutting himself with razors, leaving scars on his arms and chest. "When the pain got too much," he explains matter-of-factly, "then I would get rid of the pain by cutting myself with razors."

Frank now realizes his reverting to self-abuse was not suicidal; nor did he return to alcohol to numb the pain of impending loss. In this sense, he was coping in a healthier way with the trials and tribulations of life. But he also knew he would have to work through his feelings openly and directly rather than push them below the surface.

"So I owned up to Mary one night," Frank says. By explaining his feelings to her, he confronted himself. "I totally realized what was giving me the pain. It just triggered my reaction to earlier things in my life, stuff that had been there all my life." He connected his jealousy with the envy he had always felt toward his brother. His insight reconciled the conflicted feelings he had carried throughout his life. His pain was blunted, his despair softened. "I used the pain that I thought was coming from Mary to see that the pain was there to begin with. I started working with my early issues: my envy of my older brother. Patrick captured my mother when I was a kid. I was never able to do what he could do. My being able to take care of Mom when she was falling but my

105

inability to take her out and have a good time."

Exploring childhood conflicts allowed Frank to save his friendship with Mary. At the same time, he began to free himself from his legacy of loss, and with it the enduring pain of desperately trying to connect with his mother to no avail. When Mary was later diagnosed with breast cancer, Frank was there to support her as a friend. When she faced the decision to undergo a double mastectomy, he shared her terror and joined in her process of mourning. When Mary lost her hair, Frank did not reject her. He saw her beauty within. "We never let go of one another," Frank says. "We stayed friends in an open relationship. . . . She was the key that opened the doorways so that I could have a better relationship with myself."

A significant part of Frank's new, healthier relationship with himself is attributed to his therapist, his mentor, and his friend, a man also named Frank. He first met Dr. Frank while attending a workshop during his early years of sobriety. "He became my father about a half hour after I met him," Frank reveals with profuse admiration. He describes Dr. Frank as a "benevolent, old, Irish New Yorker," a man in his sixties who had an illustrious career as a narcotics detective much earlier in his life. Dr. Frank later become a psychotherapist, developing special expertise using psychodrama techniques in alcohol counseling.

"He has a very soft manner," Frank continues, "but you know you're always in the presence of a man who has a lot of power." Clearly, Dr. Frank has played a pivotal role in the course of Frank's recovery. He has helped Frank develop a deeper understanding of his unresolved emotional issues while consistently supporting Frank in the process of opening up and taking necessary risks.

An important risk has been a willingness to work on painful issues through the process of psychodrama. As the name implies, psychodrama involves emotionally expressive and often spontaneous techniques that enable individuals to dramatically confront past, present, and future dimensions of their interpersonal fantasies and experiences. Through this unique form of therapy, a sort of therapeutic theater, Frank was able to experience powerful catharsis. Dr. Frank provided the safety Frank needed to incorporate these insights into his recovery, and the emotional release propelled Frank forward in his healing journey.

Along the way, Frank discovered he had something to give back to others as well. Through the openness and mutual support of the group process, Frank found that he could help people who identified with his pain, his struggle, and his persistence. In addition to AA and ACoA meetings, Frank became active in a small support group for people who had survived suicide attempts. The group followed the twelve-step tradition, but in many ways seemed different to Frank. He found that the group members were not afraid to openly share and confront the pervasive fears, fantasies, and impulses associated with suicide. Frank describes the group as a safe haven "where people could come in and really talk about their fears, their yearnings at that time for death. It helped me because it did things that no other meeting ever did. It allowed me to say I'm here because I attempted suicide. . . . And there were no secrets. We weren't afraid to listen to the word 'suicide.'"

Reflecting on the bond shared by suicide survivors, Frank emphasizes the importance of using time as a resource. "People who are recovering from suicide attempts have an agenda that other people don't. We need time to do things. We need time to get our heads together, our hearts together, so we can stay alive. We're coming from another space, and we have to allow ourselves time to do the work that's really important. We have to invest enough time in staying alive first." Reflecting more personally about his own perspective on time, Frank continues: "I'm very slow. I do things very slowly. But once I start getting something accomplished, I don't let go of

107

it. I can't dance, but I will some day."

Frank went back to school to learn about counseling people struggling with alcohol and drug addiction or perhaps those contemplating suicide as the only way out. He takes evening courses in alcohol counseling in addition to working his full-time job as a clerk for a Manhattan law firm. It will take years to complete the rigorous course of study and extensive training required to become a certified counselor, but Frank remains optimistic that he will eventually be helping people in the way his therapist and mentor Dr. Frank helped him. Now forty-nine years of age, Frank jokes that he may be a "geriatric taking care of geriatric alcoholics." Nevertheless, he feels confident that his persistence will pay off. "I love working with people. I know I'm capable of doing real things to help real people."

In considering the tremendous responsibility of counseling people who are contemplating suicide, Frank seems almost philosophical, reflecting years of lessons learned from pain, loss, and despair. He relates a story that, for him, illustrates the significance of facing suicidal fears and impulses openly and directly, not running from them.

Embedded in the wish to die is a desperately misguided need to live. "I can quote from a part of Othello where this character wants to die," Frank says. "He's an older man and his son, who's dressed up as a helper in this scene, brings him out into a field at night. The man is blind, and he tells the old man he's at the edge of the cliff and to do what he has to do. So the old man jumps. He's only in a field so he's not going to fall very far. But in that jump, in that attempt, he literally thinks he's dead. And when he comes to, he sees his son for the first time. And he realizes that it was his son who was with him all the time and it wasn't a cliff. But he experienced the death that he needed. Like in Zen, it says, die now so you can have the rest of your life to live."

Confronting our own suicidal selves is perhaps one of the

most difficult tasks we face in life, Frank reflects. "There's a part of us that gets so intense with our self-hatred. And wherever that's coming from, that's the part that has to go—some part of you that's really a hate relationship, a shame-based relationship with yourself. But you have to find it. You have to take a chance and witness your own fears, witness the fear that's inside of you.

Suicide is a narrow experience. It's constricting. If people are in the zone of suicide, they're in a tunnel. It's hard for a person who's going to kill themselves to try to step back from a situation when you're engulfed in it. And it doesn't allow you to see anything. It doesn't give you enough insight."

Likening the narrow tunnel of suicidal thinking to a constricting hypnotic trance, Frank emphasizes the importance of breaking through an indifference to life, shocking one's critical senses with what Frank refers to as an "outrageous act." As he explains it, "you have to break into their trance. They're taken hostage by their own trance. You have to get them out of the hostage situation even for a minute and give them another look at life from a different perspective.

"That's how psychodrama has become so important in my life. You can do an outrageous act, and in doing that you can get the rage outside. You can externalize the rage that's going to kill you. You're between terror and rage, that's where you are. That's where you place yourself when you're going to kill yourself. You're between terror and rage. So your rage is the murdering portion, but the terror holds you until you're so vulnerable that you're terrorized and so enraged at the same time that you're in conflict. If it was just terror, you'd run. If it was just rage, you would act out. But when you're terrorized and enraged at the same time, you're entrenched in this frozen pit of hell but you're so enraged that you have to take it out on yourself. So you have to release that rage and you have to explore that terror."

Exploring the terror and releasing the rage—the willingness

to do these two things has been the core of Frank's recovery. Toward that end, psychodrama has provided a powerful, effective medium for Frank to accomplish them. In addition to his work in various twelve-step programs, Frank has been receptive to exploring new belief systems which have enlarged his vision, opened new doors, and created more options for coping with life's demands. Hatha yoga, guided imagery, massage, dreamwork, I-Ching, even witchcraft have engaged Frank's curiosity and helped him to explore his terror and release his rage.

In his experiential pursuit of new and different perspectives, Frank has become increasingly certain he is the architect of his own recovery program. "You have to stretch your emotions, your mind, your heart, and your soul," he advises. "You have to stretch to meet yourself, and you have to get out there and learn more. And you have to become more. The more expanded you are, the less chance you will have to kill yourself. It's when you contract, when you start getting very narrow-minded—that to me is a worrisome time. Know when the suicide run is starting again. Get to learn those feelings; get to learn the suicide signals."

In his ever expanding exploration of inward growth and outward experience, Frank has become acutely aware of his own suicide signals, the most powerful of which is his fear of loss. "Loss, the inability to function as a normal person," he explains. "I have a terrible fear that I'm . . . inadequate . . . not enough. At the bottom of it is a terrible fear that I really don't exist, that I am nothing, invisible . . . that I make no concrete impression on the world at all. That's scary." When that paralyzing terror of not existing is fueled by a rageful urge to make an impression on the world, suicide becomes the only way out for Frank.

On a brisk autumn weekend in upstate New York, Frank gathered with two dozen strangers to experience the Native American rituals of cleansing and transformation promised by the shaman Black Elk at the Stone People's Lodge. Frank admits to being skeptical and resistant initially. But there was something intriguing, and at the same time intimidating, about the presence of Black Elk, a medicine man of the Sioux nation. Dressed in a flannel shirt and chinos, he stood six feet tall with broad shoulders and rough-hewn, weathered features. Black Elk struck Frank as quietly imposing.

Following Black Elk's instructions, the group labored together all day to construct the sweat lodge that would be used for the ceremony later that night. A pit was dug inside the lodge of woven tree branches and tarpaulins. Wood was chopped. Stones were carefully placed inside the fire pit, eventually to be heated to white hot incandescence. Frank had difficulty maintaining his attention to the intricate, tedious task of creating hundreds of prayer bundles—tiny pouches of tobacco in cloth tied with colorful ribbons. These prayer bundles would be used for the evening ceremony.

As night fell, cold and crisp, tired worshippers huddled closely inside the cramped confines of the sweat lodge. Black Elk and his assistant led the ritual of prayers and chants, calling for the spirits to join the group. Inside the sweat lodge the heat intensified as the hours passed and the ceremony progressed. Frank recalled the sweat pouring from him in torrents, his thirst never fully quenched by the water passed around the circle from time to time. He lay close to the dirt floor trying to capture whatever cool breath he could find in the thick dry heat. The heat became suffocating when water was poured over the hot rocks. Smoke and steam spewed forth, searing Frank's face and burning deep into his lungs with each breath. He recalls the sensation of his body becoming white hot like the stones in the fire pit.

The cleansing ceremony completed, a pipe and portions of meat and vegetables were passed among the celebrants. Frank emerged into the brisk night air and suddenly found himself rolling around in the cool wet grass. "I was like a puppy that

111

night," Frank recalls. "I jumped out into the night. I was rolling around in the dew. It enlivened me."

While the experience was emotionally and physically intense for Frank, he would not form any specific or useful insights until his psychodrama workshop the next weekend. Before his session, Frank recalled picking up a small stone. He held it in his hand and rubbed it between his fingers. "As I'm rubbing it," Frank explains, "I felt the coolness and the hardness and the smoothness. I gave it to Dr. Frank. He warmed it in his hand for a few minutes and gave it back to me. . . . I held onto it. It was only then I realized how connected I was with my father's corpse all my life. It brought me right back to the funeral, and I was there as a boy. What I was doing was I was rubbing my father's face and it was hard and it was cold and it was smooth. And I was trying to rub life into it. I wanted him to come back again.

"I had to be opened up in the sweat lodge, to get the steam in, get the heat back in, get the life back in. And it brought me back into that feeling. I had been holding to that for all those years, trying to get some warmth into the corpse. But what I remember about the funeral was being there, trying to wake him up. Trying to wake him up."

In the cleansing heat of the Native American sweat lodge that night, Frank was awakened. Frank grew to understand his desperate effort to wake up his sleeping father, to bring the warmth of life back into his stone-cold corpse. And in confronting the risk of his own death, Frank discovered the warmth and vitality of a life renewed.

The healing journey continues for Frank. In facing life, he has discovered the strength to explore the limits of his terror, to risk the release of his impotent rage. With determination and a deeper understanding of himself, Frank can finally let go of the cold hard stone, letting it drop to the ground as he moves forward in his life.

7

Dead Serious, Dead Certain

> I have learned that success is to be measured
> not so much by the position one has reached in life
> as by the obstacles which he has overcome while
> trying to succeed.
>
> —Booker T. Washington

Perched on the edge of a dark wooden mantle above the red brick fireplace, the "morning kachina" doll stood as a silent sentinel protecting the inhabitants of this warm and peaceful Tennessee home. Painted with subdued desert colors and adorned in rough cloth and feathers, the carved wooden figure reflected the primitive craftsmanship and deep spiritual tradition of the Hopi Indians.

Holding true to Native American beliefs, the Hopi craftsman

intentionally designed the doll with a small but detectable flaw. This imperfection would establish that this was an object produced by human hand, setting it apart from the perfect creations brought into existence by the omnipotent spirits which controlled their world. In this way, the Hopis believed, human beings maintained humble reverence for the sacred by avoiding any pretense of or proximity to perfection.

Ken and his wife, Madge, the imperfect inhabitants of this home in a Memphis suburb, discovered this exquisite kachina doll during one of their many journeys to the Southwest. Sitting next to the doll on the mantle, a resplendently feathered sacred pipe served as a ceremonial reminder of Madge's distant but cherished Cherokee roots. A red clay pot occupied a special place in a nearby room, its surface decorated with a holly berry vine in bas-relief, reflecting Cherokee symbolism in a carefully handcrafted effort by Madge's cousin Anabelle.

These precious Native American artifacts, collected by Ken and Madge over the thirty years of their marriage, were carefully preserved and proudly displayed in their home. They stood as the symbols of serenity, peace, and spiritual energy they have painstakingly nurtured and renewed in their relationship. Ken, with distinguished specks of gray in his ruddy brown hair and an attentively groomed mustache, converses in a soft-spoken but deliberate manner. Subtle inflections of a southern drawl punctuate his carefully weighed words with a conservative, articulate, controlled posture. In sharp contrast to her husband, Madge appears more effervescent, with free-flowing speech and pronounced mannerisms. Madge compensates for her shorter stature with high energy, quick directness, and an expressive face accentuated by dark eyes that sparkle when she laughs.

Nestled in a quiet residential neighborhood near the cemetery where Ken's mother was buried, their home reflects the refined southern hospitality that characterizes Memphis. A major port in the Mississippi Delta, Memphis was called "the place of good abode" by Andrew Jackson in the 1800s. In recent years, the city has been known as the "birthplace of the blues" and, of course, the final resting place of Elvis Presley.

Ken's home has been Memphis since he was two, although he often wonders whether he ever really felt a secure, connected sense of home. Although his formative years were spent in Memphis, Central America was his actual birthplace. Ken was born in 1944 while his father was stationed in Honduras as a public health officer for the U.S. government.

As the oldest of three children—Ken has a younger sister and brother—Ken always felt much was expected of him, in fact more than he could ever fully attain. Recalling his schooling in Memphis, Ken notes that he was a driven child. "My identity was studying. When I saw things about bookworms, part of me identified with them. I didn't want to look like one, but there was a part of me that understood that my life was very narrow, very sheltered."

Ken's father was a prominent physician in the Memphis community. He had achieved multiple successes early on in his academic and medical careers. From as early as four years of age, Ken remembers his mother pointing out to him how successful his father was. He was touted as one of the youngest medical students at the University of Tennessee Medical School and even set records for academic achievement. "I believe my mother was trying to make me proud of my dad," Ken reflects. "But I remember the way I took it was different. I took it that I'll never do as well as my dad. To me it seemed unattainable. And so that's been clearly a wound that I have identified with for a long time and have had to make peace with in my own way."

Coupled with the compulsive, almost perfectionistic, pressure to achieve more that characterized his school years, Ken became increasingly aware of a pervasive and intensely painful performance anxiety, which at critical times was the

115

source of significant emotional turmoil for him. He vividly recalls the first failing grade he ever received. It was his first year of high school. "I was in Latin class and I'd gotten one of my first F's that I'd ever had in my life. My overwhelming sense of shame and failure was, my gosh, I cannot go home and show this to my parents. This is horrible. I don't know what this is going to do to me. I will have to just go home and consider killing myself."

The sense of personal devastation from having failed to attain perfect grades continued to plague Ken throughout his high school years, but he learned to hide it from the outside world. Instead, he internalized his performance anxiety as self-doubt, along with an ever growing pattern of self-defeat that often incorporated self-destructive thoughts and fantasies.

As a senior, Ken was encouraged by one of his most supportive teachers to audition for the school play. He was shy, but reluctantly agreed. Much to his consternation, Ken was chosen for the lead role in *Cheaper by the Dozen.* Yet he could not allow himself to feel the sense of accomplishment. "I was again devastated," Ken says, "devastated by performance, devastated by trying to memorize and learn lines. For the week before we actually went on for a one-night performance in our high school auditorium, I went to bed suicidal, thinking, I'm not going to be able to do this . . . I know I'll just have to kill myself. I don't think a single living soul knew that was what was going on in my head at that time. And I didn't know how to reach out to anybody." Even the ovation that followed his outstanding stage performance would not be sufficient to quiet Ken's critical inner voice.

Following his high school graduation, Ken remained in Memphis for his first year of college, never having been away from home. He met Madge while waiting to be inoculated at the college infirmary. "I didn't know whether I liked her or didn't like her on first meeting," Ken admits. He knew he was drawn to her in some way, but he was struck by the differences between them. Madge was attending school hundreds of miles away from her hometown of Shreveport, Louisiana. Compared to Ken, she seemed more assertive, more independent, more forceful, and more social.

Ken recognized an enduring spiritual strength and emotional resiliency in Madge that was missing in himself. "There's a part of me that's still a scared adolescent," Ken professes now, more than three decades later. Looking back, it is clear that, as a seventeen-year-old college freshman, Ken's inner anxiety and growing uncertainty about himself were already beginning to undermine his emotional bonds with Madge.

During his college years, Ken's self-doubt adversely impacted his career path. "I really struggled with what I wanted to do," Ken recalls. "I really thought I wanted to be a minister, maybe. Thought I wanted to be a lawyer. Different things. But I kind of gave in, almost in desperation, because the answer didn't come to me quite fast enough. By the time I was about to graduate, it was kind of like, well, I better just conform and decide to be a doctor. And I remember feeling real trapped by that."

Pursuing the lofty, seemingly unattainable, goal of becoming a doctor like his father triggered the crippling performance anxiety that continued to plague him. Yet he remained silent, unable to communicate these fears to those he depended on for support and encouragement. During this same period of academic transition, Ken was just beginning to face some of the common experiences of becoming a young adult. He describes himself as a "late bloomer" and a "sheltered child." Raised Southern Baptist, Ken did not begin dating until his senior year in high school, when, as he perceives it, "girls found me." As for experimenting with alcohol and drugs, Ken developed a reputation as the "designated good guy" in college. He was the straight-laced fraternity president who could be counted on to be responsible and in control. "I

117

just had no intention of doing anything wrong like drinking or smoking marijuana or any stuff that people did to test their wings or go through the natural breaking away," Ken recounts. "But my first drink was in my freshman year, and it was significant. It was a milestone in that I did love the stuff, deep within me. And what I loved about it was that with a drink under my belt, I was able to go out and dance at my first cousin's debutante ball that night. I felt like some hole within me was literally filled. Man, I could socialize! The anxiety went away, no doubt about it. Interestingly, I didn't start drinking much at all during college."

Following college graduation, Ken married Madge and settled into the chaotic life of a new medical school student at the University of Tennessee in Memphis. From the start Ken knew that his decision to attend his father's alma mater was a mistake. "Part of me had known that I probably needed to leave Memphis," he says. "I had never been away from home. I was a town student, and I was feeling quite trapped. It just didn't feel right. This is my dad's school. It was not helped by the fact that the second day in class the chemistry professor hits my name, which is a name that stands out, and he says, 'Oh yeah, yeah, I know that name. Are you Frank's boy?' In front of two hundred other students. And he said to me then, 'You know, son, you'll never equal your dad's record.' I'm thinking, I've known this since I was four years old. But it was a sinking sad feeling. It confirmed one of my deepest wounds, and anxiety was clearly in the way."

The anxiety Ken faced as a first-year medical student was compounded by major changes occurring in the medical school program at the University of Tennessee during that time. Despite his academic success, by the early months of 1966 Ken had decided to leave medical school. The decision seemed to be the right one at the time, but the prospect of taking a time-out to redefine his sense of direction did not immediately relieve his inner turmoil. "I was not moving toward anything. I was only moving away with no sense of what I was moving toward."

Feelings of guilt and failure were magnified. Ken began to contemplate suicide. Armed with the rudimentary knowledge of a medical student, for the first time, Ken's self-destructive thoughts revolved around overdosing on medication. He was not yet ready to act, but he knew he could see the path more clearly. Suicide was a way out of the panic and intolerable pain.

Ken began teaching math in a private school in Memphis, while Madge continued the teaching career for which she had prepared in college. "I absolutely loved it," Ken reflects enthusiastically. "Another defining moment, because after teaching for a year and a half, from that moment on I have mostly taken an identity as a teacher first. . . . There's a part of me that's been a teacher ever since." Both he and Madge were happy with their teaching positions and, Ken says, they seemed truly compatible and connected in their marriage.

But this idyllic period of peace and serenity did not last. As Ken explains, "the compulsion to be a doctor took over again." He had not resolved his yearning to attain the unattainable, to achieve at the level of his father's success. Can I be as good as my dad? was the question that haunted Ken, compulsively drawing him back to the study of medicine.

Against stiff competition, Ken was accepted to Vanderbilt Medical School, a small program located in Nashville more than three hours away from Memphis. He and Madge moved to Nashville in the fall of 1967. Ken remembers his initial feelings facing medical school again. This time he was away from the safe confines of his hometown. "I was terrified . . . my first time away from home really," Ken reflects. "Madge had already made those breaks and gone through those stages. Part of my debt to Madge is, she supported me in my growing up enough to be able to know what it's like to be away from home. But, as I look back on it, I was still very much an adolescent who didn't have a clue about that."

In his struggle to contain his overwhelming anxiety Ken found himself experimenting with sexual fantasy and substance abuse. He began drinking more openly, more excessively. He also discovered certain pills that diminished the emotional pain. "My dad being a doctor, we had a lot of stuff around. I grew up with a mindset that if you have something, just find the right chemical that might help it."

Empirin with codeine seemed to help. "There was no doubt in my mind, even then, that I was using it to numb enormous anxiety and absolute fear," he recalls. "And the fear was that when I got back to the same point in medical school—with anatomy and biochemistry where I had just come apart—I just knew I had to gut it out and get through it. And gut it out and get through it meant stay high as long as I could. Just keep the pain pushed down with codeine. I'd learned about it years back as something that mellows you out."

As with most addictive patterns, the "protective" chemicals Ken began using to control his anxiety would eventually threaten his health and well-being. To complement his drug addiction, Ken had also begun to fuel a compulsive fantasy to experiment with what he refers to as "mood-altering women."

Ken acknowledges the difficulty of talking openly about his history of extramarital affairs. This difficulty is not just his inability to understand why or how this destructive process could happen. After all, at that point in time, his whole life seemed out of control. He was moving rapidly toward an abyss of addiction that had the potential to destroy everything meaningful to him, including his marriage. Ken's sensitivity to talking openly about his affairs is based first and foremost on his need to protect the privacy and the integrity of Madge, who became the ultimate victim of Ken's destructive sexual compulsions.

Throughout Ken's many years of suicidal depression,

Madge experienced a private emotional struggle. She was forced to come to terms with her own frustrated relationship needs, learn to understand and accept Ken with all his faults and frailties, and affirm and validate her own spiritual and emotional strength. It was this strength—a combination of her Cherokee ancestry and a special commitment to God—that saw her through. In the end, she and Ken survived with their marriage intact.

Ken's first affair occurred during the early years of his second attempt at medical school. Looking back, he realizes that this breach in his marital commitment was the result of his inability to accept Madge for "who she was and how she was." Ken explains, "The seeds of uncertainty were there even with our first dating. Madge wasn't quite who I wanted her to be . . . but I also decided I was going to change her so she was right for me and then I'd be okay. And so when we went off to medical school, I realize looking back, I was already very much looking. I mean, there was a part of me that had moved from fixing Madge to finding, in quote, the 'fantasy woman.'"

He found this so-called fantasy woman in their apartment complex. She would subsequently become another dimension of Ken's mood-altering addictive pattern adding to his increasing alcohol consumption and his experimentation with various pills he encountered as a medical student.

With medical school drawing to a close, the impending anxiety of deciding on an internship loomed large. Ken found himself facing another period of confusion and despair in his continuing ambivalence about becoming a doctor. What in the world am I going to do with this? he remembers wondering plaintively. "All I wanted to do was to get a degree. I was ruling out every speciality rather than ruling in something."

In the midst of this career confusion, Ken's extramarital involvement was becoming more emotionally complicated. Rather than providing pleasure and comfort, it was now generating its own conflicts. As Ken recalls, "The woman was very serious. I think she was interested in divorce and a relationship. I know today that wasn't what I was interested in at all. There was a part of me that said, Wait a minute, why is she upset? I mean, I'm happily married. You know, I just wanted the affair, the mood-altering component to it."

When the woman subsequently took an overdose, Ken's fantasy bubble burst. "It scared me to death," he says, "jolted me to a reality that said, Whoa, big mistake; I think I'll pull out of that. I think part of me even said, I don't think I want to do that again."

But this first affair would not be Ken's last. His self-destructive cycle was spiraling deeper and wider as he became enmeshed in the increasing uncertainty of his medical internship. After his initial plan for a surgery internship, Ken found himself drifting back toward internal medicine, "which again put me trapped right back doing what my dad did," he explains. "It was like there was a part of me that wanted to avoid the same path and ended up right there with him."

Running from his career ambivalence, Ken attempted to transfer to an internship in pathology. However, he continued to experience the anxiety that threatened to consume him. Faced with his first autopsy on a child—a child exactly the same age as his son—Ken was flooded with dread, paralyzed in his ability to perform as the doctor he would never be.

"I couldn't do it," Ken recalls. "It was pretty much in the middle of the night, I think, when I was called in to do it. And so I got in my car, my little VW Beetle, drove out on the expressway, and took my first overdose. A rather benign overdose medically, an antidepressant. I'm taking ten or eleven of them and about all they did was make me almost hallucinate. I mean, I didn't die, and here I am sitting in my little car thinking, what do I do now?"

Somehow Ken was able to safely drive back home. Rather matter-of-factly, he told Madge what had happened: "I felt suicidal and I took some pills. I don't think it's hurt me much." In retrospect, Ken observes, "I guess that's where we both were in denial, and I didn't want to reach out for help. What I did was put it under the guise of a lot of confusion. Stress. Depressed. Not sure what I wanted to do with my life. And I just hit a crisis. But I hid the fact that I had taken an overdose. I mean, it was clearly the magic line that says, No, you cannot tell this. Because if I went that far, somebody might intervene and say, 'Son, you need some help.'"

Ironically, confronted with his first significant suicide attempt, yet unwilling to seek appropriate help, Ken decided to pursue a speciality in psychiatry. Ken describes the internal dialogue that led to his decision. "I decided to have a consultation with myself," Ken recounts, "and it went along the lines of, Okay, be honest with yourself. You've got some kind of a little problem. You've got your ass in a crack here and you don't know what you're going to do. Why don't you look at psychiatry? And for all the wrong reasons, mostly wrong reasons—the right part was that it was similar to teaching—I decided to pursue a residency in psychiatry."

Ken and Madge moved back to Memphis where, after a brief stint working with his father in the clinical research center, Ken began his residency in psychiatry at the University of Tennessee. Shortly thereafter, their twin girls were born in April 1972. With three young children, Madge was busy with her responsibilities as a full-time mother. Ken's medical career seemed to be back on track, and he had returned to his familiar hometown turf of Memphis.

But the inner turmoil continued to plague him. Although his drinking had intensified by this point, Ken was still able to hide the extent of his chemical dependence from the outside world. "In fact, I hid most of my pill and alcohol addiction pretty well for a long time," Ken recalls. "But when I started residency, I now had a license to start experimenting; and I had, in my mind, an obligation to find out what pills felt like for my patients. That's exactly the way I reasoned it."

123

Armed with this convenient rationalization and his increasing knowledge of psychotropic drugs, Ken's pill addiction was in full swing. He was in the process of completing a successful psychiatric residency, with two tours of duty as chief resident, when he found his second mood-altering woman. She was someone he could depend on to distract him from the performance anxiety he experienced as a doctor. "I especially wanted to make sure that she was with me when I was on night call in the medical center," Ken notes. "That was the roughest. That was where I had the most sense of fear and inadequacy. I would be the most out of control and vulnerable because I'm on the line in the emergency room." That relationship ended with the completion of Ken's residency and the beginning of the next phase of his career.

With a partner, he opened a private practice in January 1975. At the same time, he was continuing his connection with the university as an assistant to the residency director in the psychiatry department. By this point, Ken was ingesting increasing numbers of pills a day while still trying to treat patients. With those patients who were addicts themselves, Ken found himself faced with the personal and professional dilemma of trying to convince these patients to cease using the same drugs to which he himself was addicted. These were the same drugs that were making him more depressed, impairing his mood, clouding his judgment, and distorting his self-image.

In the midst of this fog of addiction, Ken began another extramarital affair. Unlike the others, this one became a significant long-term relationship, lasting much of the next eight years. "That's longer than a lot of marriages," he notes. "During those eight years she got a heck of a lot more of my energy, my time, than Madge ever got." Just as Ken rationalized his experimentation with drugs to support his projected need to be more competent professionally, he also explained away his guilt about being unfaithful to Madge, emphasizing the need to protect his adequacy and ensure his happiness. "See what you made me do!" he would angrily confront Madge when her suspicions were raised. "After all, the mind-set had been that Madge was the problem all along. If she had been the right woman, I wouldn't have done this stuff."

Despite his defensive denial and projection of blame, Ken's facade of professional adequacy was insidiously crumbling under the weight of overwhelming anxiety, depression, anger, and guilt. All the emotional ingredients for suicide were there. On August 13, 1976, the obsessive thoughts of ending his life finally reached a crescendo of impulse and action. On an isolated road near Brownsville, not far from Memphis, Ken once again found himself sitting in his car waiting to die. This time he was far more conscientious in his drug selection. He deliberately chose one of the most lethal drugs available, and in a toxic dosage. A massive quantity of an antidepressant, double the minimum lethal dosage, he felt sure this would be sufficient to complete his last merciful act as a competent doctor. There was nothing left to live for, Ken reasoned. He would simply be easing the suffering of a hopeless patient who had exhausted all of his resources. He was dead serious, dead certain that this attempt would not fail.

Ken's recall of events surrounding that suicidal overdose are still hazy. He did everything right, he thought, but nevertheless failed to complete the job. At some point he remembered stumbling out of his car when two young children happened by. The paramedics eventually arrived and transported him to the hospital where he remained in a coma for the next three days. After multiple resuscitations, Ken woke up to face the intensive care staff in the same Memphis hospital where he worked.

His first feeling was anger. He remembered trying to fight off the efforts of the nurse who was attending to his intravenous line. There was absolutely no sense of relief in waking up alive, only anger that he had failed and that people were frustrating his efforts to die.

As a psychiatrist, Ken knew how to play the role of the good patient. Successfully hiding his drug addiction, his affairs, and his secret obsession with suicide, he 'cooperated' with those who were trying to treat him. Within a short time, he convinced his caretakers that he was sufficiently recovered to resume his professional duties. "But within three days of going back to my practice, putting the white coat on," says Ken, "I was back to using fifty pills a day. I was back in the relationship, trying to keep it going. But part of me knew that I was destined to do the whole thing again. I was just marking time. In that interim period was when I lived just horribly suicidal."

Over the next six years, Ken remained actively but secretly suicidal. As he remembers it, "probably not a day went by that I didn't have thoughts about suicide. It would be worse if I were in between supplies of drugs. I would definitely feel trapped and desperate. And I'd be withdrawing at that point, so I'd feel like hell and I think I would get more suicidal. A new supply comes in, I'd probably ease off on it a little bit, putting it off for awhile."

Ken fantasized about jumping out windows and driving into bridge abutments. He flirted with the use of guns and thoughts of hanging himself, trying to muster the nerve for another suicide attempt that would not fail. Above the recessed ceiling tiles of his office, Ken had rigged a noose attached to a heavy metal pipe.

"Periodically, in my anger, my rage, and my desperation, I would go in my little biofeedback lab where I had all this rigged up and see if I could get up my nerve to hang myself. It was kind of like a ritual." On one occasion, Ken's rehearsal nearly became his final performance as he slid the noose around his neck and kicked the stool out from beneath him. "Somehow my neck came out," he recalls. "I woke up a few seconds, or minutes, later. I didn't tell anybody—I still had my white coat on—and, I think, went home."

Ken's last suicide attempt occurred on a cold winter day in 1982. Looking back on the circumstances surrounding this attempt, Ken knows that this crisis was the result of accumulated conflicted emotions crashing down on him. Further compounded by drug-induced distortions that clouded his perceptions of himself and others, the triggering event was his distorted reaction to Madge's decision to return to teaching.

It was the morning of her first day back to school, Ken recalls. There was the typical commotion of everyone pressured to get ready for the day. "Madge made a harmless comment. She looked at me and said, 'Now you see what it's going to be like with me teaching again.' Now, I know she was referring to the chaos of everybody getting up and all the confusion. But my mindset was so distorted by that time, I took that as the last-straw attack and affront on me. I guess I heard it as, 'See what you created.' Obviously I carried so much shame and guilt, most of it secretive, that I heard that as an attack. And that was the triggering event. I was enraged. I started that day in a process which ended up with the overdose."

Ken found himself locked in a trance, focused down the narrow tunnel in his mind with only one thought and one goal: to kill himself once and for all. But this time his planning and his approach were not as well thought-out as the last overdose. Rather than carefully choose the most lethal drug, Ken impulsively decided to overdose on medication he had taken away from a patient. Ironically, this was a young man who Ken was concerned might be suicidal and might use the medication to hurt himself. "This attempt was much less lethal, maybe more desperate and less thought-out," Ken says. He readily acknowledges that this last overdose was indeed a cry for help.

The combination of barbiturates and Dilantin that Ken ingested that day left him sick, but alive. He was admitted to the neurotrauma unit of the hospital where he worked. This particular combination of medications and the resulting hospitalization began the process of detoxifying his body from the drug addiction that had consumed him for so many years. At this stage, Ken was still hiding his addictions. Protecting his secret compulsions continued to prevent him from reaching the source of his pain. While recovering in the hospital, he was finally confronted with his avoidance and the self-defeating nature of his evasions when a female ward clerk asked him, "Why don't you let some of us help you?" Surprised by his sudden tears, Ken finally realized that for years he had been running from the help he so desperately needed but was afraid to request.

"That was indeed a defining moment because for the first time, honestly, I said, My way isn't working. I'm not going to try to hide, pretend, or whatever. I'm willing." Ken was finally ready to accept help. He allowed himself to be admitted to the psychiatric unit where he practiced, the same unit where he had made rounds on the day of his overdose.

After three days in the unit, Ken recalls, it finally hit him that his healing journey would only begin when he was ready to accept help, to allow his secrets to surface, and to face the commitment to living life. Ken remembers this insight as a "lightening bolt type of thing, a truly spiritual experience, that, my gosh, here I had tried multiple times—two times fairly sincerely, one time dead seriously, if you don't mind the pun—and yet I survived. And it was the first time, I remember kind of looking up, thinking, There is some kind of higher power, some kind of a reason. I don't know what it is, and I don't know what life has in store for me. I've never forgotten that."

From the hospital in Memphis, Ken's healing journey transported him to Dallas, Texas, where he admitted himself to the Timberlawn Psychiatric Institute, a nationally prominent program providing intensive, highly structured and often innovative treatment. Over the years Ken had referred some of his own patients to Timberlawn and had come to trust and respect the program. But he soon found that, as a patient in a psychiatric unit, he was forced to develop a whole different dimension of personal trust. This trust would begin with self-disclosure rather than emanate from the staff or fellow patients. This painful process of self-confrontation and openness would slowly unfold for Ken over the next nine months of his inpatient stay.

On his second day at Timberlawn, Ken found himself connecting with a California woman who was struggling with learning to use crutches and a walker, part of her own physical rehabilitation from her suicidal leap off the San Francisco-Oakland Bay Bridge. "I think even at that time I knew that this would probably be somehow good for me, to help someone else. So we would walk and talk together, at times trying to help her with her walker and talk about what it was like. We talked about the shame of having something happen that immediately puts you in front of the public like a suicide attempt, and how to start dealing with it."

This kind of "reaching out by reaching within" was just the medicine Ken needed. It became an integral part of learning to trust himself and others. Giving of himself allowed Ken to lower his barriers and access the healing resources he needed to work through the Timberlawn program and prepare for a return to the world he had left behind. Looking back at the program, Ken says it became a safe place where he could "surrender to some kind of process and trust."

Ken was soon disabused of the notion that this would be a quick fix—just play the role, follow the rules, and you will be home free in thirty days. Through intensive individual therapy and a multitude of groups—many of them based on a twelve-step model—Ken worked hard to plumb the depths of his addictions; to shore up his crumbling defenses against the inner terror, rage, and guilt that haunted him still; and to

129

begin repairing what was left of his fragile self-respect. "There's no doubt about it," Ken declares emphatically, "the hospital and the experience for that length of time changed me. When I finished there I was not the same person who went in."

September 10, 1982, brought Ken back to his vulnerable core. The cascade of terror returned the day Ken was discharged from the hospital to return home. "Timberlawn had been the first place I could emotionally connect with as home. That was really frightening for me to realize that even though I grew up here in Memphis, that I'm not sure at a deep, deep emotional level I ever had a sense of home. So at Timberlawn I had a sense of home, and the separation of leaving there was absolutely terrifying to me. A little part of me—the little emerging sense of who I am, that I definitely learned at Timberlawn—was there. And parts of me could only be described as an extremely terrified little boy inside."

Ken notes the irony of this self-revelation. "I was already a psychiatrist. I was thirty-eight years old at that time. And yet I had just embarked on a journey of barely understanding at an emotional level who I really was."

Pausing to reflect on this critical juncture in his life, he struggles to contain his emotions. "E.T. was the movie that year. I saw it five times. The real connection for me was when little E.T. would point his finger up and say, 'E.T. phone home.' I would pour tears that I didn't understand at first. But part of it was my connection with an idea of home that was both a found joy but a tremendous sadness at what I believe today was never having connected with that way back in childhood. So I identified with little E.T. Man. That was me., that was me."

Ken continues to fight back the tears as he relives this powerful emotional connection to his childhood. The transition period he encountered in leaving Timberlawn and returning to Memphis became important in strengthening the connection to his wife. "Madge was with me," Ken recalls. "All I could do was to say what in AA is called the third-step prayer: Thy will be done. I must have worn that out a thousand times a day. Each mile that we drove back to Memphis, I could feel—literally—some life force leaving me that I felt I was leaving at Timberlawn. I was terrified, and I think at the deepest level I was terrified of suicide. There was a little voice in me saying, Oh no, is it all going to start again?

"I know today that I still had the option tucked away in the back of my head, that I had made no real peace with some part of the suicide thing. I'd worked on it, talked about it. I'd agreed that I'd been angry about it. I'd done a lot of emotional work, but cognitively it was still there. It was still there in this way: If all else fails, meaning all the treatment, all the Timberlawn, all the twelve steps, well, I can always kill myself. That was the holdout. That was the option. It had been there since about the ninth grade as best I can identify today."

Ken worked diligently, almost obsessively, on his aftercare. He attended twelve-step meetings daily, remaining zealously sober while desperately trying to keep the suicidal mounting pain and terror at bay. Early in the dark hours of a brisk October morning, his first day back to work as a doctor again, Ken found himself staring that final option of suicide in the face once again. "Five a.m., I'll never forget it. I was making my meetings. I had worked my steps. I had done, 'all the right things,' and there it was. I woke up primarily wanting to hang myself in the attic, or I could get one of our shotguns. And I was terrified. I was devastated, just panic-stricken, because I knew it was now a moment of truth.

With a flood of emotion that he previously would have hidden behind his expertly crafted facade, Ken decided to take a risk. He picked up the phone and called his sponsor. "I went downstairs because I didn't want to scare Madge to death. I'd scared her so many times with all my suicide and acting out stuff. I said, 'Well, Stan, this is Ken. I hate to wake you up, but let me get right to the point. I'm just sitting here wanting to either blow my brains out or hang myself.' I said, 'It's interesting. I don't want to overdose this time because that would mess with my sobriety, and I'd rather die sober.'

"Crazy thought," Ken concludes, "but it was very serious." Supported by the compassionate, firm direction of his AA sponsor, Ken was encouraged to "suit up and show up," to take the step that was immediately facing him and return to work that day. He was advised to talk more openly and honestly in his group meetings and to share his suicidal thoughts and not just to talk about his addictions. In opening up, Ken found that others were more willing to share their own pain, terror, and guilt. "Outside the hospital, it was the first time that it had been talked about meaningfully," Ken notes. "To confront the shame and pain right here and now, face-to-face with people . . . But I think that was a huge step that I had to do for my own healing at that point."

This critical step would soon be strengthened by a crucial insight. As Ken was attending his regular meeting, listening to one of the speakers, he happened to glance up at the list of twelve steps prominently displayed on the wall. He found himself focusing on the third step: "Made a decision to turn our will and our lives over to the care of God as we understood him." This was the formal version of the shortened third-step prayer Ken had repeated over and over to himself on the drive home from the hospital: "Thy will be done."

Ken read the third step several times before it finally hit him. "Because what I was looking for I suddenly realized wasn't there. That step did not say a word about turning my addiction over to the care of God. The words 'will' and 'life' absolutely jumped off the page at me. And I thought, I haven't done that. I don't know if I ever can do that. But that's a little bigger job. It's not, I'll turn my drug problem or my alcohol problem over to God. And if that doesn't work I'm not going to give you anything else. All of a sudden, I realized it was my *will* and my *life*. That's everything, as much as I can give."

Ken was stunned. This insight forced him to reassess his whole defense system. Realizing that it was based entirely on the illusion that he could regain control of his life by trying to shut out any and all thoughts of suicide, Ken recalls, "it dawned on me at that point, it hit me throughout every part of me, that I could feel. That after all the suicide attempts, I was still there. All my best efforts, my very best efforts—and I didn't make half-assed efforts in my opinion—I had not died. And that had to be for only one reason: there's some kind of purpose, some kind of force out there that says, nope, nope, not yet.

"It wasn't my life. I didn't make me. And I believe this in my soul of souls today; I won't determine when I leave this life as we know it. Up to then, I thought I could, and desperately needed to think that I could control this life and especially this death (meaning the way I could exit). And so it hit me very powerfully. Call it a surrender if you want. If I try, it isn't going to succeed unless some kind of force other than me means for it to. . . . Our task is only to start seeking what the purpose is, what's the meaning."

For the first time in his life, Ken was forced to confront a totally different concept of personal control. It required seeking the larger purpose, the meaning to his life rather than just fighting off or denying the suicidal thoughts. "Within about five days, I woke up for the first time since the ninth grade and knew, beyond a shadow of a doubt, that I did not have the suicidal thought tucked away any more within the back of my head, the thought that if all else fails, I can kill myself. It was gone. It has not been there since. It just simply has not been there.

"People ask me sometimes, 'Are you absolutely, 100 percent guaranteed sure that you will never kill yourself?' And I answer it about the same way I do my addiction:

Conceptually, I believe that if I did not take care of myself—
that is, to work one day at a time and do things to stay on a
journey of recovery—that I would slip back to old patterns,
including addiction. And I fully believe I could get back to the
point of being suicidal or attempting suicide. I know I'm capable of that for sure. I've been there."

Ken explains the fundamental change in his perception
this way: "In the past, I only had a mode of defending against
the world. Or I had a strong sense of What can the world do
for me? What can I get from it today? Can I get a bunch of
pills from it today? Can I find a woman to mood-alter with
today? It was take, take. And I know today that I was very
self-centered. I was a desperate man trying to fix myself. No
doubt about that. But the key to me today is that I'm in some
way giving and seeking."

Giving and seeking. These are the beacons that light the
way on Ken's spiritual path, providing the impetus and the
direction for his healing journey to continue. And Ken's journey is Madge's journey as well, for Madge has been there with
him every step of the way. She has had to face the demands of
her own anguish and has worked hard to discover her own
sense of meaning and purpose in life. And she has found the
strength to recommit herself to her marriage.

Madge's experience is both unique and typical when compared to the experiences of others close to a suicidal individual. For Madge, it was frustrating to continue rowing the boat
while Ken jumped overboard and floundered in the stormy
sea. His self-destructive compulsions threatened to capsize the
whole family. Tossed about in her own tempest, buffeted by
fear, anger, guilt, and depression, Madge was continuously
challenged to remain steady, stable, strong. Herein lies her
unique gift.

Madge's spiritual strength can be attributed to a combination of her inherent Cherokee wisdom and a special "covenant
with God" reflected in her marriage vows: "Let no man put

asunder." These were the words she clutched as her anchor, helping her to remain steady and helping to carry her and the children through those trying years. For Madge, her journey of recovery has been guided by what she refers to as "spiritual footprints": trusting in God, trusting in herself, and ultimately learning to again trust in Ken.

Trusting Madge's strength has been an important dimension in Ken's recovery as well. "Madge is absolutely a miracle, in my opinion," Ken states. "She has a strength about her, a very deep emotional strength that I'm learning to have. My strength, as I see it, has become more in the spiritual area, as I'm learning to grow emotionally. Madge believed in me deeply and saw something in me before I had any hint of anything there. I'm deeply grateful for that and I still count on it today."

Ken's validation of Madge's spiritual strength has been important to both of them in their efforts to redefine the marital bond. They have reached back to the core of their early relationship—those first young years as college freshmen—to find the healthy connections upon which they can rebuild their marriage. Incorporating the "one day at a time" principle, they have both committed themselves to exercising daily the option of deciding to stay in the marriage or opt out, thus preventing the marital trap. Rather than strengthening the walls of the fortress that surrounded the marriage, Ken and Madge are nurturing the spiritual energy that provides the inner strength they need to remain close and connected.

Ken cherishes the spiritual energy he and Madge seek in the world and share with one another. Madge's heritage has contributed greatly to this spiritual energy. "She has always had very deep Native American values," Ken observes, confessing, "I didn't grasp or appreciate them at all in the early years of our marriage. I just kind of knew she had some Cherokee blood and that was it. I'm getting caught up to speed with the Native American spirituality that Madge has known and been taught by her elders since the time she was a child. And yet, she has never had places outside of the close connection with Cherokees where it felt safe for her, for people to appreciate what she knew and believed in. And so it's been absolutely a bridge that we have begun to connect with, when she could see that I truly began to connect with and embrace Native American values and wanted to learn more."

In addition to providing a spiritual bridge for the marriage, Ken's newfound immersion in the study of Native American powers and principles has allowed him to formulate a more personal and meaningful sense of God. He explains, "The Native American tradition deeply touched me. It expanded my God. The Native Americans have an expanded sense of God by incorporating a lot of nature: That man is not somehow up here and all other forms are below, but that we are all one. That we are God's children, in a sense, of all things in creation. And that really touched me. It appealed to me. It's part of why I love to travel today. I love to connect with the nature and the spirit of tall trees, and I have come to believe in and connect with the energy forces and things that occur from very sacred places. To me, that's the spiritual journey."

Ken's expanded sense of God has also allowed him to change his perception of who he is in his relationship to this higher power. "I grew up in the Southern Baptist Church," Ken explains. "I took on a God that I choose to have a very different view of today. But the God I took on in my early formative years was extremely stern, extremely judgmental, virtually nonforgiving. A God of hellfire and brimstone. The first images I used in recovery at Timberlawn were that he was a God with six shooters. I mean, he sits up there and all he's doing is waiting to shoot at me with that first screwup."

Through his connection with the hospital chaplain at Timberlawn, who encouraged soul-searching and self-discovery, Ken began to question and challenge his long-standing conception of God, asking, Is that really the full nature of God? "I continued to view God as powerful," Ken says, laughing that God "had a great deal more power than I did over killing myself." His perceptions have since undergone a drastic transformation. "Amazing changes, in my opinion, just in the way I experience God," he explains. "As I began to be much less shaming of myself and judgmental and hard on myself and driven, interestingly, God began to be a lot lighter and more loving, more forgiving, more supportive, more funny." Ken acknowledges that this "lighter, more loving" view of God was the same image that Rosie, his family's life-long maid, had conveyed to him as he was growing up.

Rosie came into the family when he was nine years old. "Truly my black mama," as Ken describes her, Rosie helped to raise him as a child and to this day remains actively involved in his own family with Madge and their children. When Ken was at his most critical stage of despair, Rosie was there for both Ken and Madge, with solid guidance and strong spiritual beliefs. Ken readily proclaims, "Rosie saved my life. Without her I'd be dead today." Incorporating the image of Rosie's God, Ken's renewed faith was expanded by the Native American values and new beliefs he and Madge were exploring in their spiritual quest together. Integrated with the twelve-step tradition, the values of the Episcopal Church, and his work in traditional psychotherapy, this supportive combination has formed the multidimensional recovery process Ken has lived for the more than fourteen years since his last suicide attempt. "They have helped me synthesize my spirituality so it begins to feel more like a nice consistent whole," he says. "They were all different parts of me when I started, and the journey has been how to make peace and bring those together to enrich and let me grow."

Helping him make sense of the emerging parts of himself is his therapist, Ted, a psychologist who has been treating him for the past thirteen years. Ken describes Ted as a unique individual, a "spiritual man," someone he could trust to understand and channel his most private, most painful thoughts and feelings. With the support derived from intensive individual therapy and his twelve-step work, Ken has continued to explore the roots of his addictions and the depths of his suicidal obsessions.

This search has taken him into other therapeutic experiences over the years, including ACoA support groups to work with childhood issues, Sex and Love Addicts Anonymous (SLAA) to explore his sexual compulsions, and a weekly men's group. Ken is also involved with the Impaired Physicians program in Tennessee which has allowed him to play an active role in physicians confronting other physicians about their own chemical dependency.

Seeking and giving constitute the central focus of Ken's recovery. Seeking answers to his own questions about himself has been integral to expanding his role as a caring person as well as a helping professional. "When I got to twelve step," Ken cogently explains, "one of the principles there is you can't give away that which you don't have. That rang a bell with me. It went back to old analytic principles which said basically you better work on your own analysis before you're going to be ready to help other people."

More than just giving lip service to this aspect of his professional identity, Ken has worked to integrate self-discovery and self-disclosure into his practice as a psychiatrist. "I'm known as someone who understands sexual addiction," Ken explains. "So I do a lot of work in that area. I do a men's group for male sex addicts, many of whom had suicide attempts and who had chemical dependence and other things. And so there's no doubt that my career has largely been defined by just staying on my own journey. I just do my journey, and then I'm kind of pulled forward in my career."

Ken continues to view his career as dynamic and evolving, following the progression of his own journey of recovery. In addition to his private practice, he currently serves as medical director for trauma services in a multi-care psychiatric hospital in Memphis. His professional responsibilities allow him to work with people who are dually diagnosed with both chemical dependency and psychiatric disorder.

In his work with suicide survivors, Ken is cautious about disclosing his own history. "I do answer questions about myself when directly asked and I think the person is really ready to hear. What I find is that generally they will move much faster in being able to talk about that dimension of their life. There is a sudden sense of freedom to talk knowing that they're talking to someone who understands. And there's no doubt that at many levels I do understand as much as anyone understands this whole thing about suicide." But with careful qualification, Ken adds, "I don't think I have all the answers to my own story. It's an ongoing work in progress, as far as I'm concerned. But at least there is an immediate bond that says here's someone who's been there and understands."

Ken has little doubt that he is becoming a more effective psychiatrist and a more balanced doctor as the result of his own recovery process. With an eye to the future, Ken observes, "It feels like the next part of the journey for me personally is more healing around suicide. . . . I only know that I haven't finished healing and I've got more work to do." Recently Ken has taken the initiative in founding a support group for suicide survivors. Modeled after the twelve steps, the burgeoning program functions as a Suicide Anonymous group, where people can talk openly and share their personal experiences. The group process provides a kind of mirror in which people can see more of themselves through the experiences of others who have made the same journey to the edge and back again.

Ken readily acknowledges that beginning a project such as this represents a major risk. At an earlier time in his life, this kind of ambitious thinking would have threatened to disrupt the precarious balance of his fragile ego. "In the past I'd have had to be dead certain," Ken says, wryly referring to his fear of taking risks. Now he is more willing to accept his vulnera-bilities and limitations, incorporating them into his ongoing process of living and learning, giving and seeking.

In his continuing search for greater understanding of him-self and his emotional connection to his loved ones, Ken's jour-ney recently carried him back to his birthplace in Honduras. It was the year of his fiftieth birthday. He and Madge had just returned from a trip to Europe, a trip that celebrated the renewal of their marital commitment. This was the "fulfillment of a promise," Ken explains, one of many promises to Madge that he had broken over the years of their marriage.

Exhausted from their travels, he and Madge were looking forward to settling back into the peace and quiet of their home life when they received a phone call from their son in Jackson, Mississippi. Their son explained that he had an opportunity to accompany a group of Baptist missionaries on a trip to Honduras. The invitation was extended to Ken and Madge, as well as to Ken's father who was advancing in age.

In short order the trip was arranged. Spanning three gen-erations, the entourage flew to Tegucigalpa, the capital city where his father had been stationed in the 1940s and where Ken was born. Ken describes his father as "a young whipper-snapper—twenty one, twenty-two years old" at the time. "He went down on his own, not speaking a word of Spanish, and my mother joined him. . . . It's very clear that every time I hear my dad talk—and when my mother was alive, we'd hear her talk—of quite happy times. My pictures were all of a happy child at that point." Ken pauses briefly, then reflects with cha-grin, "Interestingly, if you look at my pictures at about age three to four, there's no happiness."

Ken can recall only vaguely his childhood memories with his parents in Honduras. But he is acutely aware of the signifi-cant differences between him and his father at similar points in their medical careers. The image of his confident young father stands in stark contrast to memories of his own confused and highly conflicted transition to adulthood and an ever elusive professional identity.

Ken remembers his emotional reaction when the family disembarked from the plane at Tegucigalpa: "I was just kind of weak-kneed. Wow! This is literally the mother earth! This is where I was born. I was consumed immediately with an image of the house that we had . . . a gorgeous old Spanish-type house."

Ken and his father were drawn, almost spiritually it seemed, to find the house that remained only an uncertain image in their minds, faded by time like an old photograph. His father, still fluent in Spanish, began asking questions of those who lived in the area near the elegant Honduras Maya Hotel where they were staying. Finally, one of his father's contacts came through. A surprising phone call brought them the news. The man on the phone told them to look out the front door of the hotel. Located directly across the street was the house where Ken had lived with his parents fifty years before! It had been converted into shops, but the house was intact, just as they had remembered it.

Ken and his father were overjoyed at their luck. "And it turned out that Madge and I had picked the room that also looked right over it. That's where I had lived. I mean, we were spellbound. And it was powerful and important to me. There's a part of me that now knows my deepest roots and felt them by going back there."

Seeking to learn more about his roots, connecting more profoundly with the happy times from his early childhood, and reconnecting more intimately with his father, his son, and his wife—these were the results of Ken's nostalgic journey back to his birthplace. But something was missing. His mother was absent from the family portrait on this pilgrimage to the past. She had died in 1985 following her third heart attack.

Ken still grieves her loss. Memories of his mother's death conjure scenes from his grandmother's death many years earlier.

Ken felt particularly close to his grandmother. She died when he was fifteen or sixteen, "and it was my first death that I had really remembered clearly experiencing," Ken explains. A heart attack also was the cause of his grandmother's death, adding to the longstanding history of coronary artery disease in his family. "My dad also has had both bypass surgery and a mild stroke, so I definitely have the heart problems on both sides," Ken says.

It was April 24, 1991, a Wednesday evening, Ken recalls, when he experienced the pressure in his chest, the tightening in his throat, and the pain radiating into his jaw. He had just finished playing his usual game of tennis, the same doubles game he had played every Wednesday evening for years. Madge immediately noticed his agitation and pacing when he arrived home. Ken's medical training did not dispel the wall of denial, but Madge insisted he get checked out at the hospital only five minutes away.

They were met at the emergency room by Mike, a close friend and cardiologist Ken trusted. The electrocardiogram gave them the bad news: at the age of forty-seven, Ken was having his first heart attack. "I remember thinking, You've got to be kidding! Forty-seven years old? I thought about my mother. Thought about my dad, my grandmother. The nitroglycerin eased the pain somewhat, but the abject terror was still there. Ken turned to his trusted friend for reassuring advice.

Angioplasty was recommended. This was an invasive procedure. A ballon-tipped catheter is snaked through a groin incision and carefully worked up to the coronary artery blockage. The balloon is then inflated, creating an enlarged opening in the artery that allows blood to flow more smoothly, which restores the heart to a more healthy functioning. Usually this kind of procedure necessitates a sedative. Ken's strong devotion to his recovery principles held out, however; he was carefully monitored throughout the procedure without sedation. The angioplasty was successful in opening up one of the two vessels that were blocked. Almost immediately, Ken's excruciating pain subsided, and he was admitted to the coronary care unit just before midnight.

Ken vividly recalls that first night in the CCU when Madge reluctantly left. The doctors pronounced him stable, but still in critical condition. The nurses were busy with their nighttime routines. He found himself alone in the subdued light, with a lidocaine drip, monitored by a maze of machines noisily proclaiming their presence with flashing digits and colorful lights.

"I was terrified," Ken remembers. "I knew I was having arrhythmias. They'd warned me that the first night would be the roughest. . . . I mean, I'm bright enough as a doctor to know arrhythmias mean the whole thing could shut down. It could go haywire, and I could be out of here. But along about two o'clock in the morning when I was pretty scared, just plain scared, I had for a brief instance an experience that was kind of like in my eyes. It would be like if you suddenly had the white dots, you know, of a flashbulb that leaves the white. But my eyes were open. And there was an energy that just totally pushed me back in the bed. I knew beyond a shadow of a doubt it was some kind of higher power. I've never forgotten it."

Over the years, Ken has learned to pay careful attention to these experiences, which he has come to call "white light moments." From all his reading, Ken knows these are not exactly like near death experiences reported by others. But he is dead certain these are powerful and important life events that must be taken seriously. He is convinced they serve as a profound wake-up call, a message sent to him from a higher power.

"I've come to realize that I'm much more scared of living

than I am of dying," Ken observes, readily admitting he has always been scared to be a doctor. Through these white light moments, he confronts his deep-seated anxieties and long-standing fears of living life to its fullest. These silent signals are constant reminders that he must continue to expand his life, despite the risks and uncertainties, that he must seek a life full of meaning and purpose in his professional identity as a doctor, and that he must continually challenge his self-centeredness and self-doubt by giving more of himself to others.

For Ken, as well as his spiritual partner, Madge, this quest for meaning and purpose through seeking and giving has added precious value to their lives together. "Until death do us part" no longer serves as the ultimate threat to their marital bond. In facing life and death, Ken and Madge have discovered a more durable strength, a more lasting commitment, and a special inner peace that nurtures their relationship.

8

Shouting from the Rooftops

It was a particularly difficult delivery, Martha remembers, more painful than she had been led to believe in her childbirth classes. The birthing room at University Hospital in Cincinnati was set up to promote comfort and composure. She remembered using the rocking chair, and the warm shower certainly helped during later stages of her twenty-three-hour labor. Diane, the attending midwife, provided sensitive and soothing guidance to Martha, supporting her desire to give birth without any painkillers. Martha's husband, Alex, proved to be a more assertive coach than she had anticipated. Despite the physical and emotional support she received, however, the excruciating pain and extensive blood loss proved traumatizing.

Martha felt incredibly weak and shaky as her first and

only child, Zachary, was coaxed kicking and screaming into the world at exactly 11:32 a.m. on Tuesday, August 6, 1991. Initially it was hard to cuddle him in her arms, Martha recalls. She felt afraid she might pass out and drop the precious child she wanted so desperately to hold and protect. She wanted to never let him go.

Becoming a mother was a "terrifying decision" for Martha. "Probably the hardest thing I've ever done in my life," she says. More terrifying than the risks of giving birth, more difficult than facing the demands of mothering, the decision to bring a child into the world required her to make a firm and lasting commitment to being alive. "I had to decide I wasn't going to kill myself before I could decide to have a child," Martha explains. That meant Martha was finally giving up the many years of searching for ways to end her life. It also signified her readiness to assume the role of a devoted and dependable mother who would be there for her child for as long as he needed her. This was a promise her own mother did not fulfill. Martha was only twelve years old when her mother finally succeeded in killing herself.

Looking younger than her thirty-five years, Martha's intermittent nervous laughter seems strangely out of place, particularly as she relates moving depictions of growing up under the cloud of her mother's suicide. Tears would certainly have been in order. It becomes readily apparent that Martha draws from a resource of vibrant energy within herself which defuses her underlying sorrow and cynical anger. With strawberry blonde hair flowing off her shoulders and hugging her face, Martha projects a bright and cheery demeanor. She speaks spontaneously and rapidly, perhaps too quickly to adequately convey her thoughts at times. The resulting flow is often halting and dismembered, punctuated by her infectious and disarming laugh.

Martha misses her mother terribly. She would have liked her to be at the hospital for Zach's difficult birth. The first night home with her newborn, Martha was terrified when he would not easily awake to nurse. Her mother might have provided the reassurance and emotional support Martha needed at these critical times. Zach proved difficult to breast-feed. A problem with his palate frustrated his sucking reflex, leaving him incessantly demanding, and Martha's nipples painfully raw. Her mother's presence would have eased Martha's concerns while nurturing her confidence in becoming a good mother herself.

Later, Martha may have turned to her mother for guidance in dealing with Zach's increasing behavioral problems. After raising four children, including Martha, her mother certainly would have listened to her frustrations and shared her experiences. Perhaps Martha today would not be questioning and blaming herself so much for the strong will and opposition displayed by her physically active and demanding four-year-old son. If her mother had not killed herself, if she had committed herself to staying alive, Martha's life as a lonely child, a troubled teenager, and a new mother might have been much different.

"I really miss my mother," Martha repeats. "We had something very special. She and I had this thing called 'M & M,' which was for 'Mommy and Martha,' and we'd talk. My mother was very easy to talk to. She was able to help me find words for my feelings."

Perhaps because of this special bond between them, Martha reacted particularly strongly to her mother's first suicide attempt when she was six years old. She vividly recalls that her parents were "fighting, hitting each other, screaming, and yelling.". The details of her mother's attempt to kill herself remain vague, shrouded in a fog of family secrets. Martha only remembers, "When I was six years old I stopped talking, except at home. By the time I got into first grade, I was so shy I wouldn't talk. Away from home, I would answer a direct question, but only in a whisper, unless it was to defend

147

someone else."

The contrast between the shy silent child she was then and the effervescent adult she has become is striking. Reflecting back to those early years of staying close to her mother, being afraid to leave her alone, Martha now knows she was trying to take care of her mother as much as, or more than, she was protecting herself. "There was a sense of death in my house," she recalls. "I kind of knew something was always wrong." Martha's childhood memories are disorganized, but remain strongly defined in their emotional impact. "When she was in the hospital following the first suicide attempt, we had this maid who took care of us and used to beat us with this hairbrush. We were all afraid to tell my father."

There were many things Martha felt afraid to tell her father. A prominent New York physician and specialist in nephrology, Martha's father was excessively involved in his work, rigidly intellectual, and emotionally detached from his family. He lacked warmth, empathy, and compassion. "He's a very good doctor," Martha admits. "His father credentials aren't too good, but his doctor credentials are great." She punctuates her impression with a hearty laugh, pauses briefly to reflect, and then continues in a more serious vein. "I think there was a sense of incredible deprivation in our home, emotionally. I remember having this doll, and I used to sing to the doll that nobody loved me."

With the sense of impending death surrounding her mother and the emotional deprivation contributed by her father, Martha's retreat into silence became a necessary part of her defense system. "I don't know that it was a means of survival as much as I felt that nobody wanted to listen," she reflects. "I was afraid of their response and also that I did not have the words to express what I felt."

The deprivation and withdrawal worsened when her parents separated. Martha was probably nine at the time. The escalating conflict and emotional confusion that preceded the separation were difficult for a child's mind to understand. Many years later, Martha's memory remains clouded. "There were some things prior to my father actually moving out. Prior to that suicide attempt when my mother was hospitalized in a coma, when she beat herself up or my father beat her up. To this day I don't know what happened. I remember the police coming. And my unwillingness to say my father beat my mother up kind of alienated me from my mother's side of the family. They wanted me to go into court and say she was beat up by my father, and, quite honestly, it was perfectly possible. But I didn't know for sure what really happened. I already had an overdeveloped sense of right and wrong. Even though I wanted to live with my mother more than anything, I couldn't bring myself to lie."

Martha's voice was silent. She could not talk to anyone about the emotional turmoil surging within her. She could not speak her mind. Martha recalls the stormy custody battle waged between her parents that left her and her siblings caught in the middle, unsure what would happen next in their chaotic family life. Her mother's chronic depression and repeated suicide attempts allowed her father to successfully petition the courts to retain custody of the children. Following the suicide attempt that left her in a coma, her mother was discharged against medical advice and was taken back to her parents' home in Kansas.

Martha vaguely recalls a period during which she and her siblings were "kidnapped." Her mother was desperate to hold on to them, as the custody battle seemed irretrievably lost. "We went along willingly because we wanted to live with her," Martha explains. "We lived in Kansas for a while until my father got permanent custody. My grandparents were unable to use us as pawns to get support money from my father." Eventually, the children were returned to their father in New York.

Her mother's last suicide attempt proved successful.

Martha was twelve when she was told that her mother had died. She remembers it as "a family secret, in the sense that my mother was cremated before we were told she was dead," she explains. "My grandparents didn't want anyone to know she'd killed herself, but we all knew she had. And to this day I don't know where her ashes are. I never saw her body."

For Martha, this lack of closure interfered with the normal grieving process. "I remember my dreams going through this whole series of her being alive and then not being alive." Martha jokes with sarcasm, "It was a bad time for my mother to kill herself." The loss of her mother was extraordinarily painful, the end of the special relationship they shared.

Following her mother's death, Martha's voice returned. The shy, silent withholding that had consumed her from the age of six with her mother's first suicide attempt was dramatically lifted when her mother died. "Perhaps out of desperation or because I felt I had no other choice, I didn't start talking until my mother died," Martha reveals, "and I haven't stopped talking since." Rather than colluding with the family secret that shrouded her mother's suicide, Martha suddenly found herself talking openly about it to anyone and everyone who would listen. "I mean, my response was like, Yell it from the rooftops!" Martha adamantly explains. "I idealized my mother. I felt like my mother was right. . . . I remember telling people that it was the world that had killed her, that she was this wonderful, sensitive person and the world had killed her. And so I saw the world as the enemy."

Speaking out became Martha's characteristic way of asserting her independence as she exploded into adolescence. This resulted in open and frequently volatile confrontations with her father. "I was extremely defiant," Martha admits without a shred of remorse. "I had trouble keeping my mouth shut."

She recalls the summer after her mother died. Facing not only the sudden loss of her mother but the loss of her childhood as well, it was a particularly difficult period. "I was in some kind of weird state," Martha notes. "I was not a child in the sense that I was already developed, and I was not really girl-like. And I wasn't good at getting people to take care of me because I was always the responsible one, the one who takes care of everybody else."

Martha remembers actually occupying her mother's chair at the family table, positioning herself as an easy target for her father's unresolved anger toward his deceased ex-wife. By the age of thirteen, her flagrant defiance of her father's cold authoritarian control moved beyond simply speaking her mind. Martha began to act out more openly in school, challenging authority and rebelling with her peer group.

Her self-image drastically changed within a relatively short period of time. "I went from being probably the kid who was considered like the shyest person in the whole world . . . who would never do anything wrong, or certainly never do drugs or be promiscuous, to be overnight—" Martha pauses abruptly, searching for the right words. "I made friends fairly easily at that point. I didn't start using drugs until I was fourteen, but when I started getting involved in being really self-destructive, I would make friends with people so I could get drugs. Not a real friendship thing."

By the age of fourteen, Martha's premature efforts to establish her independence were expressed primarily through self-destructive behavior. Rebellious acting out with drugs and promiscuous sex would presage a tumultuous period that extended into her late twenties. Thoughts of suicide reflected the same morbid view of the world that she identified with the plight of her mother. "The world was this horrible place," Martha somberly reflects. "Most people would ask, 'Why would someone kill themself?' And I would go around questioning why anyone would want to stay alive."

The drugs that Martha used became an integral part of her questioning the worth of living, as opposed to the seductive temptation of dying. "Basically I would take anything," she confesses. "I mean, I was never addicted to anything because my purpose in taking them was not to get high. It was totally self-destructive. I used to try to will myself to die. Just lie there and will myself to die."

At fifteen years of age, on the anniversary of her mother's death, Martha made a deliberate attempt to end her life. She overdosed on a variety of pills washed down by a bottle of her father's favorite scotch. Twenty years later, the events of that night and the following day are still hazy to Martha. She remembers waking up and calling her boyfriend, telling him she had to get out of the house. She remembers returning home late that night and being confronted by her father about the messiness of her room. "He came into my room, which was what he would do, and just dumped all the stuff out of my drawers and closet, telling me I was a slob. Then after I went to sleep, the next thing I remember, I woke up in the morning and my arms were cut and I'd written on my walls in blood and marker."

This was not Martha's first suicide attempt, but it was the first cry for help that caught her father's attention. At the age of seven, the year after her mother's first suicide attempt, Martha swallowed a bottle of aspirin. "I remember vomiting and waking my little sister, who must have been four, to try to get my parents. She didn't want to do anything. So I just stayed up, and I remember my ears ringing for about two weeks. But I didn't tell my parents."

Nearly nine years later, a bloody message on her bedroom walls screaming out her pain, Martha looked to her father, her only remaining parent, for the help she needed. When her father came into her room that morning, he simply told her to call her doctor and then left for work. The psychiatrist Martha had been seeing was a colleague of her father's whom she did not like. Similar to her father dismissing her desperate pleas for help, her psychiatrist treated her suicide as "just this manipulative thing," Martha explains. "And it wasn't. I really wanted to die."

In retrospect, Martha realizes that her psychiatrist, in collusion with her father, had "tricked" her into being admitted to Paine Whitney, a renowned psychiatric hospital in Manhattan. She remembers the psychiatrist asking her if she wanted to leave the house for a couple of days. "I said, 'Yes, that's what I've been trying to do all along.' I said, 'I have to get out of here.' And he said, 'Okay. Well, you can go here and sign yourself in and you can leave whenever you want.'"

Three and a half months later, when her insurance was depleted, Martha was finally discharged from the hospital. "It was a horrible experience," she recalls bitterly. "It was a nicely decorated prison with abusive guards." The youngest patient in an adult ward, Martha found herself reaching out to others, readily sharing her pain while allowing others to express their own hidden anguish. She discovered her ability to help disadvantaged, voiceless people and, in turn, to allow them to help her in many ways. "If I could be there for somebody else," Martha remembers thinking, "maybe somebody could be there for me. Maybe if I could make it better for somebody else, maybe I could prove to myself that it's possible."

Martha celebrated her sixteenth birthday involuntarily confined in the hospital. "It was one of my best birthdays I ever had," she recalls wistfully. "Because all the patients on the floor got together and gave me this surprise party. I had no idea, and everybody on the floor chipped in. My birthday happened to be on Memorial Day that year, so there were fireworks across the river, and all day long until I went to sleep this party went on. I can't believe that a whole floor of inpatients in a psychiatric hospital were able to do that and keep it quiet."

In planning for her discharge from the hospital, Martha knew that she could not, indeed would not, return home to her father. Her adolescent defiance had not been assuaged by her hospitalization. At the same time, her father's caring and compassion had not been revived. On the condition that she apply for admission to an extended residential program, Martha was given permission to live temporarily in the home of a former camp director in Upstate New York near Woodstock. She had gotten to know Rudy and his family when she first attended his camp during that critical summer of her thirteenth year shortly after her mother's death. Martha applied to the residential program but subsequently refused admission. Instead, she remained with Rudy for the next year and applied for early admission to Grinnell College in Iowa. She attended her first year of college during what would normally have been her senior year of high school.

At the age of seventeen, Martha felt totally responsible for taking care of herself, free from adult supervision. But she also found herself alone in the world. A series of unstable connections with forgettable boyfriends, some of them live-in arrangements, would be only temporary respites from the emptiness of her life and the depression lurking in the shadows. She eventually attained her college degree, graduating summa cum laude from New York University. Martha was always considered the intelligent one in her family, teasingly referred to as "the keeper of the brain" by her sister.

Throughout her twenties, Martha continued her struggle to maintain self-sufficiency in the face of her deepening depression and compulsive self-destructiveness. Martha remembers that long stretch from age fifteen to her late twenties: "A lot of my life was looking around for ways to kill myself. All through that time I had never stopped wanting to kill myself. My suicidal stuff was a chronic kind of thing. It was more like getting up the courage to do it. If somebody could hand me a pill and say, 'You'll die if you take this, but you have to take it right now; you can't think about it; you can't do anything first,' then I would take it."

There were a number of minor suicide attempts, which

154

Martha only vaguely remembers years later, but two episodes stand out as significant. "One was very serious and one I knew I didn't want to die," she explains. At the age of twenty-two, after hoarding a variety of pills collected from friends, Martha overdosed. She desperately wanted and expected to die, but was only "knocked out for four days," she recalls. Waking up alone in her apartment, she began salivating profusely. She remembers being unable to hold her head up.

"I was terrified of being hospitalized," Martha explains. "So there was no way I was going to do anything where anybody was going to find me and hospitalize me." Confused and scared, but still alive, Martha called her ex-boyfriend with whom she had just broken up, "because I knew he wouldn't do anything." She also called the psychologist, "Dr. R," she had begun seeing. "I had an appointment with him the day I woke up," Martha notes. "I called to tell him I was sick and could not make it to my appointment." At that point, she did not trust him enough to tell him about the suicide attempt.

Martha's therapeutic relationship with Dr. R has been a continuous source of support for her from her early twenties to the present time. "Dr. R believed in me," Martha asserts. "He believed the things I said and he just genuinely likes me." He helped Martha to overcome her "inability to trust reality" by validating and supporting her feelings and experiences. "I remember him telling me once that he felt that I was one of the best reporters of reality that he'd ever encountered," Martha adds.

This close connection with her doctor was critical in Martha's life, and likely reduced the severity of her last suicide attempt at the age of twenty-six. Martha acknowledges that it was a deliberate attempt, but quickly notes that "somehow it felt different. I wasn't as sure I wanted to die. But I don't know that I consciously said, I don't want to die." She remembers "kind of lying down to die and thinking, just knowing, I wasn't going to die . . . that somehow this wasn't going to happen. I knew I wasn't going to die."

While this final half-hearted attempt did not signal a strong will to live, Martha clearly realized the ambivalence she felt about killing herself, despite her lingering depression. The absence of this heavy obsession with suicide felt like a weight had been lifted from her shoulders. She could begin to see herself and the world in a different way. Separating herself from the suicidal bond she had with her mother, Martha experienced for the first time the true value of trusting relationships with people. With the help of Dr. R, Martha discovered a new voice. Rather than remain a shrill, futile cry of desperate defiance against a world that would not listen, her voice gave her the ability to express herself strongly and clearly, to help herself and reach out to others.

In addition to the support she received from her therapist, Martha attributed the strengthening of her voice to another man who believed in her. Sheldon became her close friend and a major promoter of her hidden talents for helping others. He was working as a reporter for a local newspaper in Hoboken, New Jersey, where Martha lived at the time. She met him inadvertently while he was researching an article on tenant organizations to fight abusive landlords. "He was one of the first people, other than a therapist, that I really talked to about being suicidal," Martha says. "Sheldon would really sit and listen to me."

Through her close friendship with Sheldon, Martha was encouraged to consider medication to help relieve her depression. She recalls her initial reluctance and pessimism. "I resisted taking medication because I thought it would make me happy when I shouldn't be. Because I believed the world was such a horrible place, and I'd rather be dead."

After unsuccessful trials with a variety of antidepressants over several years, Martha eventually received a positive result with Prozac, a new "miracle drug" introduced to the United States in the eighties. "Prozac worked for me in a day,"

Martha proclaims. "It was the most amazing thing. I remember walking outside and thinking, I've never seen the sky before. And I got angry at a lot of people. I stopped making excuses for them. The anger was empowering in a lot of ways. But the Prozac did something for me. It allowed me to not be depressed long enough to feel good and learn better coping skills for when I do get depressed."

Looking back at this early experience with medication, Martha acknowledges that the miraculous benefits of Prozac did not work consistently for more than a few years. But with a lessening of the chronic depression that had plagued her since childhood, she became less resistant to exploring other combinations of medications as part of her ongoing treatment. "When I was pregnant, I had gone off the medication, but I knew it was there," Martha explains. "There was something I could take again. Knowing that there was something to do made a difference. When I felt better, I dealt with people better."

People and Prozac became important healing resources for Martha as she gradually emerged from her dark suicidal depression. Through her association with Sheldon, she became involved in tenant organizing and rent control issues in her town. Martha discovered she was very good at "fighting for other people." Sheldon "taught me how to make myself heard," she says. "I would go to these buildings and I'd help organize. I'd walk into these rooms full of people and I looked like a little kid. Sheldon would come with me. He speaks so slowly and haltingly, but somehow his presence there allowed me to speak up. And people really believed me and I was very good at what I did and I did it for a long time. And I've met a lot of friends since then who are still my friends."

Sheldon provided the background knowledge and the persistent motivation. Martha provided the fiery enthusiasm, the zealous passion and the defiant rhetoric. These were the

157

ingredients needed to encourage people to step up and take a stand, to do their own shouting from the rooftops, to force people to listen in order to accomplish significant changes in their lives. Martha's outspoken anger on behalf of others became an important part of her own process of change, a strengthening of her own survival resources. "I feel like part of my survival was the same thing that also got me into trouble, which was speaking the truth," she observes intuitively. "Some of my shouting from the rooftops allowed some things to come to me that would not have otherwise."

Martha was appointed to the town's rent control board, an accomplishment which expanded her self-confidence. At the same time, however, it added more stress to her already hectic, pressured life. "I got really burnt out because I was called twenty-four hours a day. . . . It was a no-win situation," Martha concludes. "But I met a lot of people. I felt competent. I felt focused. I had something positive to do in the sense of making it better for somebody else." Repeating the motivation that guided her during her hospitalization at the age of fifteen, Martha adds, "If I could be there for them, maybe somebody would be there for me."

That somebody proved to be Alex. Martha first met Alex when both were young teenagers. It was in the fall of her eighth-grade year, she remembers. Her mother's suicide had occurred that spring, and she was still in the grieving process, in the core of her depression. But Martha had started to talk more openly about her feelings, reaching beyond the closed doors of her family to connect with friends who would listen. Alex became one of her friends. Over the years, they would continue to run into each other, renewing their friendship. Late in her twenties, as she was emerging from the depths of her last suicidal depression, Martha called Alex to help her manage one of her many apartment moves.

"Alex is a very nice person, one of the smartest people I've ever known," Martha explains with a sense of certainty. "I have to say, a lot of my other relationships were not with people quite as nice. It was the first time in my life when I was not depressed. I had been going through a very productive period where I felt it was okay to be alone." She had never really thought about Alex as more than a friend. But he proved to be persuasive in changing her mind. "I would never say it was this incredibly passionate romance," Martha notes. "I think I associate some of the passion to fear, I guess fear of loss. And I don't have that with Alex. I didn't think I had to work to keep him. I mean, Alex has known me through an awful lot of stuff."

It took about a year before Alex's persistence paid off. He and Martha began to talk seriously about marriage. "Our wedding was very funny," Martha reports, barely suppressing a giggle, "because we kept trying to plan it, and I couldn't deal with it. I couldn't deal with my family. So I finally told Alex, 'It's either get married or have a wedding, but we can't do both.'"

On impulse, before anyone could change their minds, Martha and Alex abruptly chose a date to get married: October 26, 1990. Within forty-eight hours, they had rounded up friends and family members and arranged for an informal country wedding at Rudy's house near Woodstock. The local justice of the peace performed the ceremony. Rudy and Mary had painstakingly crafted the wedding rings. A "huge, incredible feast was prepared," Martha recalls happily. She particularly remembers the traditional German wedding cake Rudy made for them. It was a carrot cake decorated with real flowers and topped with a unique piece of folk art that Rudy had found in his shop. The centerpiece was a carved wooden bed with an angel sitting on the headboard. The words Happily Ever After were etched in colorful letters above a bride and groom who nestled together under the covers. "Of course, I said I wanted to know if they were dead or sleeping," Martha laughs, "but that was the top of our wedding cake."

She pauses for a moment to think about that special wedding day, readily noting the similarity to her sixteenth birthday in the hospital when she was surprised by the outpouring of gifts from strangers whom she had grown to love. Somberly, Martha acknowledges the sharp contrast between her emotionally estranged family and the closeness she has experienced with the many and varied friends she has come to know over the years. In many respects, these friends have become her surrogate family. "People do incredible things for me," she observes. In relation to her family, Martha has made the decision to continue her caring *about* them but to give up her role as caretaker *of* them. "If they need me I'll be there. But in the many ways my friends are there for me my family has never really been there for me. And I love them and I hurt for them in a lot of ways. I can look at this and see all this stuff that's terrible, and it hurts. But then there's also the other side, which is that I've been very lucky. I feel in ways I'm lucky that I was so depressed. Not that that was so good, but I feel like there are things in my life that I have a better handle on now."

In her marriage to Alex, Martha has been forced to deal with their personality differences as they have faced a number of difficult adjustments together. "I'm very reality-oriented," Martha frankly professes. "As long as I know what the reality is, I feel I can handle it. But it's that feeling of not knowing. That is what occurred a lot in my growing up, this feeling of not knowing. I never knew, I mean, I didn't know if I came home if my mother would be alive. I didn't know if we'd have food to eat. I didn't know if my father would buy me clothes for school or underwear or anything. And so I'm a little bit neurotic about planning, like saving money. But I also am very—" Martha pauses for a moment, then continues her thought. "I don't lie to myself a whole lot. I'm scared of it."

Martha discovered she was pregnant soon after she and Alex were married. Alex's job as a systems analyst for a computer firm required them to move to Ohio, near Cincinnati,

160

where they purchased a home, had a bouncing baby boy, and lived for the next four years. "I hated it out there," Martha admits. "It was just horrible." She felt out of place with the midwestern lifestyle and the people, whom she perceived as pressing for conformity. "It's very, very conservative. Everybody is expected to be the same, and I'm not good at that," she states emphatically, punctuated with a laugh.

The differences between Martha and Alex were revealed most strikingly during their stay in Ohio. "He would have stayed there in Ronald Reagan country forever," Martha notes. "If I don't like something, I try to change it. I try to do something. And Alex would just choose to be content with the way things are, just accept it. It gets very frustrating for me, because some of Alex's behavior represents to me a living death, which is very frightening to me, to not engage in life, to not make your life. And for me, life is movement."

Martha and Alex and their active toddler, Zach, eventually moved back to New Jersey. They lived for a time in a cramped Hoboken apartment and then recently moved into a more spacious suburban home in Highland Park. In addition to her responsibilities as a full-time mother, Martha continues to make new commitments and explore new options. Following her personal philosophy that "life is movement," Martha remains open to pursuing meaningful goals that will engage her zest for life while lessening her opportunity to sink back into a depression. She continues to talk openly, and often publicly, about her personal experiences, helping to forge a purposeful direction for her integrated roles as a mother, a wife, and a friend.

Martha has developed a special interest in helping children work through the grieving process that surrounds the death of a parent. This interest evolved from personal experience, certainly, but it was triggered by a sudden revelation on Mother's Day more than ten years ago. "I was watching some show on television," Martha recalls. "They were talking about their mothers. And it just hit me that I didn't have a mother, that I had no idea what it was like to have a mother. It really hit me. So I called the self-help clearing house and asked if there were any groups for children whose parents had committed suicide. And they said, 'There aren't any.' There were survivors groups, and so I went to a survivors group in Brooklyn, and I met David."

David proved to be another special person in Martha's healing journey from living death to living life. From his own experiences with long-standing depression, David understood the stigmatizing dynamics of suicidal pain. He understood the shame and self-loathing, the pervasive fear and unbearable sense of powerlessness. Above all, he understood the abject alienation and dark feelings of loneliness.

Martha and David began talking about their personal experiences with depression and the absence of appropriate support groups for those who have survived their own suicide attempts. They agreed about the importance of public education as a way of preventing suicide. From the seeds of their germinating friendship, the concept of Suicide Prevention Resources was born. "We just got to be good friends," Martha explains. "I'm very good at generating excitement, and he was very good at the practical aspects. And basically we started to get grants primarily in education. The idea was to destigmatize the survivor and to destigmatize the subject of suicide."

Martha's specific interest in helping children has developed from her continuing involvement in the preventive education programs she and David envisioned. "I'm really interested in children and bereavement," she explains, "because I really believe that what happened to me didn't have to happen. I mean, I may have still been depressed, but if there had been somebody there—if somebody had paid attention when my mother made her attempts, when she killed herself—then I would have had a different experience."

Martha pauses to reflect on her anger as a child, alone with her grief. "I would like to create something where when a child experiences a loss of someone close to them systems are set where the school can call to deal with it. I've done a lot of training with people, you know, just learning to talk about that because we don't talk about that well. Grief is alienating for a child. I remember meeting this child whose mother had committed suicide when she was twelve years old. She wanted to know if there were any other twelve-year-olds whose mother had committed suicide. I was already an adult, but I went and talked to her. I listened to her, and I recognized everything she said. It was really amazing!"

These experiences of meeting, listening, and talking with people about their suicidal pain and the loneliness of loss have helped Martha to better formulate her own sense of why she survived her own suicide attempts and what her purpose for living has come to be. It has been nine years of living life since that last attempt at the age of twenty-six. Martha recalls the significant people she has met who have truly believed in her, allowed her to talk openly about her feelings and experiences, and helped to validate her perceptions of reality.

She remembers her friend Sheldon telling her, "You can't kill yourself until you go and do these important things." Martha also reflects on her relationship with Dr. R. "I remember Dr. R saying to me one day (because I was doing this rent control stuff and I was also trying to kill myself all the time), 'You know, you're really heroic.' And I burst out laughing. I mean, even though I talk a lot, I'm very shy and I would get up and talk to people. And here was this person who understood how hard it was for me to get up every day, that every day for me is something that I had to choose."

Defying death by consciously choosing to live each day does not feel like a heroic act to Martha at this point in her life. She readily acknowledges, however, that her defiance has, to a large extent, helped to vaccinate her from experiencing life as a victim. "A victim feels that everything happens to them," Martha explains, "and if I view things happening to me as opportunities or as paths or things to learn from, then I feel a sense of empowerment."

This sense of empowerment stems from her creating a connection with caring and supportive people and fashioning a surrogate family. "I began feeling competent and valuable to people," she reflects. "I mean, I met a lot of people who value what I have to give instead of telling me all the things I didn't have to give."

Martha stops for a moment to think about her choice to live life connected to caring people who believe in her. "You know, it's funny. When you asked the question about why I didn't die, I mean, maybe it would have been the world winning. Maybe it wouldn't have fit my defiant personality." This last reflection brings an enigmatic smile to her face that quickly erupts into her trademark laugh.

As the interview with Martha draws to a close, distinctive paintings that adorn the walls of her apartment become the focus. "My painting was another defiant act," Martha notes, pointing out the progression in her artistic themes and styles from early adolescence to the present time. "I started out not having faces. Actually, I never thought about that until now, but they did start out as being just blind figures. The faces developed over time. They also had no defined body. They were just cloaked."

One picture on the wall above the couch depicts a small, genderless figure huddled in the corner of a starkly empty room. The imperceptible face is averted downward, away from the window that protrudes sharply from the blank wall. The abject loneliness and despair are palpable in this example of Martha's early work. Her palette of colors is limited to muted grays and washed-out browns. Bright colors are notably absent as figure and ground merge into the shadows.

"I wanted to be an artist when I was a kid," she explains

164

pensively. "But it was the one thing I couldn't do. I mean, I was told I had no talent. I was told it was a waste of my intelligence. Painting was a defiant act and it was for me. It was like meditation. When I could really paint I felt good. It felt okay to be alone. The painting is part of that, when I kind of retreat. It is also one of the places where I've learned to accept some of my own limitations. For a long time I didn't finish things, and when I did, I often didn't show them to people. I was terrified that I wouldn't paint, that I would just be making excuses all the time. And now I show everybody what I've done, and I've sold some paintings. For me, the painting is important. Now my painting is not something that is simply therapeutic. It is a major drive, a major force in my life. I now consider myself a serious artist."

From the despondent fifteen-year-old who painted the walls of her bedroom with her own blood, to the self-assured, vibrant thirty-five-year-old woman capable of shouting her feelings from the rooftops, Martha's artwork reflects the dramatic progression of her inner growth over time. She now feels capable and competent to share her paintings with others and to talk openly, loudly, and frequently about her healing journey.

Martha can still remember the shy, scared little girl whose only voice was her primitive paintings that expressed unspeakable pain through a silent void. Martha remembers sending some of her pictures to her mother in Kansas City. "One of the last pictures I sent to her she never actually got," Martha says with considerable anguish, the pain of her mother's suicide apparent on her face. "It's a picture of a girl facing this empty road, basically the back of this girl standing alone. You can't see the face, just the road and nothing there. It's very empty because there was this road that just kept going and a field on either side of it with nothing but grass. And you don't see the face. It was a specific message, you know."

Martha stops talking for a moment and looks away, far

away, it seems, in her silent reflection. As she struggles to suppress the tears welling up, tears that briefly dissolve the sparkle of her eyes and extinguish the vibrant lilt of her voice, Martha knows exactly what message she was trying to send to her suicidal mother so far away. The painting of the faceless girl on the empty road spoke a thousand words. But the picture arrived too late for her mother to hear the message. "I was so lonely and I was so . . ." Martha, now a mother herself, cannot complete the thought as it is drowned out by an intense longing. Despite her silence, the message of the little girl comes through loud and clear.

9

Opening a Window into My World

Dear Florence and Eddie,

It feels hard to begin this letter, yet I also feel really eager to write it. The night that I called and asked you to come out here several months ago, it was with the hope of finding out from you something about myself and the years we lived as a family in the house on Westerly Avenue. . . . It feels so sad to me as I write this to really know that you knew so little of what was happening with me—just as I knew so little of what was going on with you or my sister. Whenever I picture the four of us living in that house, I always see the same image: each of us by ourselves, alone in a separate room of the house. Whether or not that is accurate, that is how it felt to me then and that is how I remember it now.

> I know that during those eighteen years I said very little about myself to you. The truth is that I said very little to anyone. I never talked to anyone, really, until I began therapy with Tom. I have come to understand the reason for my deliberate silence. It was two-fold. First, I withheld information about myself out of anger. . . . I came to know that the one thing that I had that was valuable to you were my thoughts and feelings. The only power that I had as a child was to give these to you when you asked for them or to withhold them. And I chose to withhold them. . . . This brings me to the second part of my stubborn withholding of myself—I withheld for self-survival. Anything that I did offer was immediately gobbled up by you. I literally felt like I would be devoured if I gave anything of myself. Any sign of independence was immediately squelched and discouraged and eaten up. You really wanted to keep me a child—helpless and unable to function without you. . . . You really crippled me so that I couldn't exist, but I came to believe what you wanted me to—that I couldn't live without you.

Working carefully to share these eloquently crafted words, Sharon reads short excerpts from her thirty-page neatly typed letter to her parents, Florence and Eddie. The letter was Sharon's attempt to describe the enduring pain of growing up in the emotionally barren and intrusive world of her childhood home in Delaware. Three thousand miles away in the state of Washington, ten years after her abrupt break from her parents at the age of nineteen, Sharon could finally risk communicating the insights she had gleaned from her years in therapy. Together with the emotional connections drawn from her experiences with new people she had met along the way, Sharon hoped the letter would open a window into her world. She hoped her parents would accept an honest invitation to understand her lifelong "struggle in the dark" to "emerge into an adult, happy person."

It took Sharon nearly two months to write the letter. "It was explaining my childhood as I remembered it. It was explaining how I remembered myself, how I remembered each of them, how I remembered my sister, how I saw the dynamics between us, how I saw them as parents." In actuality, she did not begin the letter with the intention of sending it. But as it developed, Sharon liked the way the words were expressed and decided that it needed to be shared with her parents. She saw it as therapeutic for herself as well as for her parents, an important part of the healing process she was pursuing at that stage of her life. "I liked how I wrote it," she explains. "I like the tone because it wasn't angry. I express anger in it but it was not a blaming letter, not an angry letter, but an honest letter."

When Sharon finally mustered the courage to send the letter to her parents, there would be no response, not even an acknowledgement of her parents having received it, for two long excruciating years. Sharing the intimate revelations of her letter more than twenty years later, Sharon is less sanguine, less stoic than she was when she first wrote it. Now she appears more in touch with her anger, more aware of the utter emptiness of her emotional life with her parents, more cognizant of their pervasive limitations.

Short in stature, with dark hair highlighting the delicate lines of her sculptured alabaster face, Sharon does not look to be approaching fifty years of age. She appears youthful, vibrant, with an engaging smile and an expressive laugh. Her warmth and sensitivity are reflected in the softened tone of her voice and her carefully articulated words, reminiscent of those that formed the message to her parents so many years before. Sharon's bright eyes intensify, her face visibly darkens, as she describes the pain of abject rejection and dismissal by her parents. "I think their lack of response was a significant factor in my trying to kill myself," she concludes. "I was hurt and I was angry. I was shocked at the lack of response and the total denial."

Within a year after writing the letter, Sharon found herself checking into a hotel in downtown Seattle. It was late in the afternoon, October 10, 1976, a fine autumn day, she recalls. Sharon remembers a cascade of tormenting thoughts that had been plaguing her for some time, demanding thoughts that were incessantly pummeling her like an "inner voice."

This voice compelled her, doggedly challenged her, to remain focused on the plan to end her life that day. It told her to act normal, to "look okay" so as not to raise any suspicions as she went about the purposeful task of collecting a variety of pills from a number of her friends. Isolating herself from others, Sharon did not want her plan to be interrupted. "I tried to cut myself off from any feelings," she recalls. "I didn't want anybody to get to me. I hated myself. I felt that I was bad, like there was something really bad that I couldn't fix. I couldn't stand myself, that's what I couldn't live with."

Alone in the hotel room, alone with her pills—a lethal load of depressant medication including Miltown, Valium, and Seconal—Sharon deviated briefly from her carefully orchestrated plan. She decided she was hungry and ordered a large, fattening meal from room service. This was to be the final pleasure she expected to enjoy before the end, the last luxurious repast for the condemned. After Sharon finished eating, the commanding voice in her head became louder and more insistent, chastising her for the delay. Go ahead, start taking the pills, the punishing voice screamed. You've had your meal. Now do it., coward! You've had your pleasure, now do it.

Sharon dutifully ingested the pills and waited for the end to come. Her memory of succeeding events is clouded by the massive dose of toxic chemicals surging through her brain, but she remembers at some point clearly saying to herself, Oh

God, this is working! I don't want this to work! This last plaintive cry did not sound like the tormenting voice that had been orchestrating her suicide attempt. Instead, this new voice sounded like herself. That was me, she thought. With what little physical strength and presence of mind she could muster, Sharon succeeded in calling for help. Close to death but miraculously still alive, she was rushed to the nearest hospital.

Waking up in the hospital after nearly thirty-six hours in critical condition, Sharon recalls her earliest feelings were not exhilaration, not even a sense of relief that she was still alive. Rather, she remembers feeling embarrassed. "I was mortified. I didn't want to see anybody. I remember that. I didn't really know how bad, how close I really came to dying, but Tom, who's my closest friend in the world—he was then and still is—I didn't even want to see him. I wouldn't see him in the hospital, I remember. And so probably the first thing I can really remember was hearing his voice over the public address system (because they wouldn't bring him in if I didn't want to see him). But once I heard his voice, I couldn't turn him down. That was, as I remember it, a very emotional reunion. And the second I saw him I was really glad. I had no real comprehension for really what had happened. I barely knew that I was alive."

Sharon's special relationship with Tom began in 1967 when she first met him in a therapy session. A psychologist, Tom was on call for her regular therapist who was away on vacation at the time. Sharon had not been making much progress in therapy up to that point. She found it difficult to trust, to open up about her childhood experiences. She was having problems adjusting in her first real separation from her parents. Far from her Delaware home, Sharon did not feel like an independent, fully functioning adult.

The separation from her parents occurred with considerable abruptness, Sharon notes. There had not been much preparation or planning. She had been living on campus at the

University of Delaware in Newark, but found herself struggling with depression in her sophomore year. The depression was intense and pervasive, making it more difficult to concentrate on her studies. Her previously high grades dropped precipitously during that last semester in the spring of 1966. More than her academic failure, Sharon remembers the emotional devastation she experienced, the painful feelings of isolation and alienation that were getting worse as time passed. "For a period of about two weeks, I stayed in my dorm room with the shades drawn, the lights out, and the door closed with a sign on it saying GO AWAY. I didn't go out for classes or for meals," Sharon recalls. "Even as unsophisticated as I was psychologically at that time, I knew that was a bad sign," she concludes.

Sharon also remembers the flood of unpredictable and puzzling tears during that semester. "Something was wrong but I didn't know what." At one point, she found herself sitting on the outside steps of the math building in an isolated part of the campus. "I remember sitting alone there for a long time, looking out onto a grassy area empty of people. After a while I started crying, quietly, for no specific reason. I continued to cry deeply for what seemed like an hour or so. Then I just got up and walked back to my dorm room. It seemed like a strange incident, but I told no one about it. For some reason I saw it as an isolated part of my life, not connected to any other part of myself."

Sharon was coaxed into seeing a psychiatrist during that critical semester, but she had difficulty initiating an open, trusting relationship with him. "As I would subsequently find out, he was not a competent therapist at all. But at that time I had no one to compare him to. Very little happened during those sessions."

Her father agreed to pay for her treatment, Sharon recalls, but he also insisted on knowing what was going on in the sessions. At one point he even called her therapist and threatened, "Look, I'm not going to pay for this unless you tell me what she's talking about." In the letter to her parents nine years later, Sharon expressed the resentment she felt about this controlling intrusion. "That just made me feel embarrassed and angry," she wrote. "That even in that situation, I still couldn't be left alone." Foreshadowing what would occur less than a year later in a lonely Seattle hotel room, Sharon confronted the distorted care and concern that she perceived in her parents' intrusions. She wrote, "I know that you were concerned, but that type of hungry concern is what was killing me off as a human being."

The summer following her disastrous sophomore year of college, Sharon accompanied her family to Washington for her grandmother's funeral. Sharon had registered for her junior year with the intention of returning to the University of Delaware in the fall, but she ended up staying with relatives in Washington. She refused to return home with her parents. This abrupt break—a desperate strike for individuation as a separate adult—caught both Sharon and her parents by complete surprise. "I had never done anything like this in my life," she confesses. "I was a very rigid person."

Sharon's letter to her parents spelled out the importance of this defiant act, a desperate declaration of independence:

> When I think back to that summer, I still am not very clear about what in me made me not want to go back home. I know that I had met a guy named Stan whom I started going out with. But I knew that I didn't really like him. He was just a barely plausible excuse to give the two of you for wanting to stay out here. In retrospect, I can remember that he was really not a very nice person to me. But I didn't even know that then. What I did know on some unconscious level was that my only hope for growing into a human being was to not go back with you.

Whatever small percent of me was alive then really did, perhaps literally, save my life. I knew that I wouldn't return home, no matter what you said or did. I felt so confused because I didn't know why I was doing what I was doing. It was the first strong independent move I had ever made in my life. I feel sad when I think of myself then because I feel like I was really brave. And many times during this past decade I have lost that energy and bravery that I felt for myself then.

Despite Sharon's abrupt break from her parents, this brave attempt to save herself would not be sufficient to prevent the suicidal crisis many years later. The loss of her bravery over the next decade would come to haunt her in that lonely hotel room, pills in hand, her inner voice urging her, Go ahead and do it, you coward! You're so cowardly, you can't even do this, can you? While courage and cowardice may have little to do with suicide, Sharon obeyed that inner voice commanding her to leave the world behind and end her life. Perhaps this was to be her ultimate and final declaration of independence.

Emerging from her stupor in the hospital, Sharon allowed Tom, her friend and former therapist, to penetrate the veil of humiliation and shame. During the course of her four years of therapy, Sharon had learned to trust Tom in a way she had never been able to trust anyone before. This process of opening up did not begin easily, Sharon recalls. "I was scared to be meeting a new person to whom I would have to try to talk about myself. The minute I saw him, though, I knew that he was different in kind from almost anyone else that I had ever met. His face looked soft and sensitive to me. I felt valued by Tom just because I was an individual human being in pain who was trying to help myself. I felt like I had finally met someone I could talk to."

Ironically, it would take Sharon nearly a year to begin

talking to her new therapist. Re-creating the "deliberate silence" that characterized her years of growing up, Sharon found herself unable to open up, to use her voice and express her feelings. "I couldn't even say a word," she acknowledges. "I wanted to. My session with Tom was the highlight of my week, and I don't think I ever missed one. I remember looking forward to my session, each time thinking that this would be the day when I would let myself lose control and really start to talk to Tom. I knew that he was someone I could trust, but I was terrified to think of really being totally open and honest with someone, to really make contact with another person. I was painfully stubborn during this first year with Tom."

Locked within her stubborn silence, Sharon had so much that she desperately wanted to share with her therapist, so much of her life that needed to be explored within the safety of a secure and supportive relationship. If only she could break through the wall she had learned to depend upon for her safety and survival. "One day, out of sheer frustration, I think, Tom actually picked me up in the chair I was sitting in and shook me—trying to shake some life into me, some movement. . . . He said, 'It's time. You have to start talking.' And then I never shut up."

Sharon laughs as she remembers the flood of pent-up feelings unleashed that day, triggered by Tom's firm but loving touch. It proved to be a dramatic breakthrough, allowing the talking part of therapy to begin. "It surprised me and scared me some when he did that," Sharon recalls. "Whatever it was about, that shaking got through to me. From that day on, I began little by little to say my thoughts and feelings to Tom. I feel so grateful to him, still, that he didn't give up on me during that year of stubborn, frustrating silence."

Over the next years of therapy, Sharon talked nonstop. She risked allowing herself to be involved in "a simple, honest relationship with a real person. I began to realize that I was developing real, genuine feelings for Tom as a person, feelings

175

that had been absent from my life as long back as I could remember. Nobody ever was interested in what I had thought. He asked the questions that implied that I was a person, and that I had thoughts and feelings and that they mattered. And I had never ever been treated like that. So I wasn't used to it. I was, like, on another planet; that's how different it was."

Through her therapy, Sharon stepped cautiously into the painful shadows of her childhood and explored her struggle to emerge from the darkness as a whole person. For the first time in her life, she began to talk about the abuse she experienced growing up in a home that provided only the illusion of caring, a fragile facade of love and nurturing. Sharon vividly recalled significant incidents in which she was treated in a "protective, destructive manner." In retrospect, these experiences seemed to be centered more on her parent's needs than on her own.

Responding to the gentle guidance of Tom's therapeutic hand, Sharon was eventually able to reveal her feelings about these protective, destructive experiences directly to her parents through the letter. "Even now I recoil if I think of you touching me or hugging me or kissing me," Sharon wrote. "What appeared to be loving affection from you to me at these times was really desperate hunger. You touched me to get something for yourself from me—not to give me anything."

Sharon learned to distrust the touch of her parents while, at the same time, not fully trusting her own perception of their intentions and needs. It would take many years of therapy and many more years of exploring her own sexuality before Sharon could begin to understand the weekly ritual of Sunday morning cuddling and tickling she shared in her father's bed.

In writing to her parents, Sharon tried to explain her confused feelings about her father's "special" way of touching her, and her mother's role in allowing it to happen:

I know that I liked it in part, because there was

such an absence of physical touching in our family, that whatever I could get I wanted. I kept coming to you at those times when you called me, almost until the time I was twelve. I believed that it was natural for us to have those kinds of feelings for each other. You were the only man I was around for many years. On the one hand it was a pleasurable experience, but on the other hand it was torturous. I felt in such conflict. I really wanted to be nice to you, a lot because I saw that you, Florence, were not nice to him. But I felt so guilty. First because of the strong implicit taboo about sex that existed in our house in general; and second because of feeling confused about my feelings about you, Florence, about your not being nice to Eddie in a way that I wanted to be—physically. Not sexually, but affectionately. So I felt both attracted to you, Eddie, because the physical touch felt nice, and also repulsed by you because of the guilt I felt. I remember in my sessions that I also felt angry at you, Eddie, for putting me in that dilemma and at you, Florence, for not being nice to him.

Her mother's intrusive, controlling touch was considerably less pleasurable to Sharon. Often her touch proved to be exceedingly painful. In the letter to her parents, she recounted the embarrassment and confusion she felt about the enemas her mother used to give her:

In retrospect, they seem uselessly humiliating to me. I remember your lying to me about them. I know that these lies were based on good intentions, but those good intentions really were destructive to me, and to you, too. They were destructive to me because they misled me into believing that the world was a painless place. But I felt confused because I thought that I was hurting. But in many

> ways, you were telling me that there was nothing
> hurting me. So I gave up my own perceptions
> because I couldn't bear to believe you because then I
> wouldn't have anyone to depend on for the truth.
> Telling those lies was destructive to both of you
> because it kept you from feeling what was painful
> in your own lives.

The pain of her mother's touch seemed less ambivalent when her mother hit her repeatedly, only stopping when Sharon began to bleed. She remembers being "eye level to the bathroom sink," perhaps age five or younger at the time. But what left a more indelible impression than the cuts and bruises were the vicious words her mother screamed at her.

Sharon heard those same savage words—"I hate you! I hate you!"—in the voice that directed her suicide attempt at the age of thirty. Sharon recalls, "From three years of age, as far back as I can remember, suicide was a clear option. I thought of that all the time. I mean, it was like a last resort that I always had. If things got too bad and I couldn't stand it, then I can at least do that. That was a way out."

Recovering from her suicide attempt in the hospital, Sharon gradually began to realize that killing herself was not the way out of her pain. As her head cleared and her embarrassment subsided, she became aware of her parents' presence in the hospital room. Alerted by Tom, they had flown out to Seattle. Later she would learn that their primary concern was not about whether or not she might suffer lasting physical complications from her overdose; they expressed concern about what she might be saying to people as she emerged from her drugged state of mind.

Sharon could imagine the questions they were asking and their readiness to defend themselves against potentially damaging answers. What did I say? she thought. Did I reveal anything when I was waking up? Did I say anything that would reflect on them? At the time of her suicide attempt, Sharon knew that her parents had received her letter the year before, but they had not yet responded to it, nor even acknowledged its receipt.

While her mother never responded to the issues addressed in the letter, her father would eventually challenge her childhood perceptions. He questioned the accuracy of her recall and denied the validity of her view of him and the family. Sharon was infuriated that they were there at her bedside, falsely professing their care and concern that she had survived. "I hated seeing them," she declared many years later in her own determined voice.

Sharon knew her immediate recovery could not depend upon reconciliation with her family. Instead, she would seek to repair her strained relationships with the Seattle friends who had become such a valuable and vital part of her life since her break from home. These were the friends she had successfully eluded in pursuing her secret plan to end her life. These were the friends she was embarrassed to face after her plan failed. And these were the friends who would become her new family, supporting her dramatically changing sense of herself.

Sharon observes that the end of her individual therapy with Tom opened a new world of possibilities for her in connecting to people. From the posture of stubborn silence that marked her initial entrance into therapy, Sharon emerged from her cocoon to become a more open, passionately engaging butterfly. She felt ready to relate to more people, to take on a larger world than the constricted life she had been leading up to that point.

During her last year of individual treatment, Sharon joined a therapy group Tom had begun. The group enabled Sharon to continue working through her difficulties openly, including her inability to trust herself and others. Encouraged to take more risks in her relationships, she began to develop more social connections and enlarge her group of friends.

As her therapeutic relationship with Tom was winding down, Sharon realized that he had become one of her closest friends. After many years of important work together, both Sharon and Tom were ready to risk extending their friendship beyond the constraints of therapy. For Sharon, this special friendship would become the catalyst for opening up to the world in a way she could never have imagined.

With new strength and determination, Sharon was ready for change in her goals. She left her elementary school teaching position after three years, completed her master's degree in clinical psychology, and became increasingly involved with a nonprofit organization dedicated to psychological education and research. Sharon was growing socially and emotionally, beginning to take more risks in her independent personal life.

In the summer of 1971, Sharon married Jerry, "the first man I was ever sexual with," she later acknowledged. Sharon had met Jerry five years before. Their relationship proved to be a roller coaster of emotional conflicts, magnifying the insecurity they both brought to the marriage. "The longer we were together, the worse things became," Sharon says. "Neither of us would break out of our own stubbornness enough to see the other person clearly and simply."

Intimacy presented its own set of problems. "I felt confused and scared," Sharon reflects. "It was very hard to admit to Jerry, but mostly to myself, that I was a woman who had sexual desires and feelings towards men. I came to feel awkward and embarrassed, unsure of myself and very unspontaneous sexually."

The marriage did not last. Sharon concludes, "We were both too scared to live alone. . . . I feel sad that this unwillingness to be alone is a large part of why Jerry and I were married." The separation proved to be more successful and less painful than the marriage, Sharon notes. It evolved as a gradual process of growing apart rather than an abrupt breakup.

"We just developed in different directions and at different rates. And he was a friend. He was one of my friends for a long time. And we remain friends." With the end of her marriage, Sharon's closeness to her friends grew stronger.

By the mid-seventies, Sharon felt secure enough to write to her parents about the growing independence and sense of belonging she was experiencing in her new life:

> I really do love living here. I love the energy and vitality and honesty and sensitivity to each other and to ourselves. I feel like my life is here now, in Seattle, living with other people who, like I am, are struggling to live our lives as independent people, capable of forming close, meaningful relationships, as unencumbered as we each can be by the painful, destructive patterns of our past lives. I feel supportive of the ideas by which we are trying to live our lives and want to share this support by struggling to live my life as honestly and openly as I can. I feel touched to realize that there are people I feel deeply for, real friends who support my independence—the live part of myself—who want to be alive themselves.

In the same letter, Sharon told her parents about Kevin, a man who would later become her second husband and, much later, the father of her two children:

> I have recently begun a relationship with someone who moved into the building this summer. I feel naturally attracted to him. I like how he looks. I like the kind of person he is. I feel respectful of his own personal struggle. And I like that he likes to spend time with me. Even in this short time, though, I can see how I am still acting out old, familiar patterns with him: wanting to be preferred,

181

to have an exclusive, safe, secure relationship with no risks involved. But I know better than to seek that for myself anymore. That kind of relationship is dead. There is no life in it. That kind of security does not exist in reality. It is an illusion which exists only in fantasy.

At this critical juncture in Sharon's life, predating her suicide attempt, the acknowledgment that she had given up the illusion of a secure, risk-free relationship proved prophetic. Despite her marriage to Kevin and her growing sense of belonging with her friends, Sharon was still haunted by her destructive past, hurt by the rejection from her parents, and emotionally handicapped in her ability to trust and protect herself. Her suicide attempt in 1976 represented a dangerously misguided effort to break free—finally and forever—from enmeshed relationships that became painful and frightened her.

Sharon's recovery depended greatly on her willingness to repair the emotional bonds with Kevin and her closest friends. Her most significant failure, she later realized, was the fact that she shut herself off from the group in order to act out her self-destructive fantasies and impulses. She failed to trust her friends enough to be open and honest with them at a time when she most needed to be.

"I was part of a group of people who hold open communication as the highest value," Sharon confesses, now nearly twenty years later. "My recovery took a long time." She quickly asks, "Is it over?" and answers, "I don't know. I think that people don't worry about me anymore. That was something that I talked about for a long time. That set up a fear in people."

Sharon acknowledges that her friendships were changed significantly by her attempt at suicide. "People were glad that I survived, but angry at me for what I had done. This was like a big event in this group of people. A huge event." Looking back on the emotional impact, Sharon observes, "My relationships with people, including Kevin, are stronger now, because we really went through something together. I didn't lose anybody in terms of friendships from this, but I didn't know it at the time. I didn't know what was going to happen, but I think people wanted to give me a chance—and they did—to try to come back to life."

Coming back to life meant coming to terms with the self-destructive fantasies full of rage that Sharon had entertained since she was three years old. "That was the biggest part of my recovery," she resolutely declares. "I knew I could never ever, ever do that again. It was not an option. And I had a rage with that. I was furious at that. It was for other people's sake. It wasn't for my own personal life that I had a feeling. But I knew that I couldn't do it again: put these people through what they went through, ever. And I couldn't make them worry. A lot of my efforts were devoted to trying to help them not worry about me, which took a long time. But that's what saved me, really. That's also what the rage was at. I hated that somebody was so important to me that I couldn't do it. More important than myself. That was my rage."

To let go of the option of suicide, Sharon had to let go of that rage. "I had such rage that I never knew what to do with it. I was so terrified that I was going to act on it. It wasn't conscious, but it was, like, in my blood, in my bones, in my body. Trying not to do this thing. Trying not to kill. And I ended up killing somebody, or almost killing somebody. I was provoked to the point that I had to kill.

"I think there's a very fine line between violence that's directed outward and violence that's directed inward," she explains, trying to distance herself from the pain. "I think there's rage that people have because of things that have happened to them. I felt like I was raised to be a murderer. I felt like a murderer. I was also raised by someone—my mother—who I felt, in retrospect, really wanted to get rid of me. She really wanted to get rid of me for her own reasons which I tried to understand sometimes, but she really, really wanted to get rid of me forever. I think she wanted me dead."

Her last statement hanging ominously in the silence that followed, Sharon pauses to collect herself before proceeding. "My mother's sister committed suicide. I never knew the circumstances surrounding it, but she did. It was her younger sister and she was an adult when she killed herself. All I know about her is that she was married, married to a doctor. She had three kids. And everything looked like it was great but obviously wasn't. I don't know how old she was, maybe in her thirties. She was relatively young. I had seen pictures of my aunt. She was really pretty. And I knew that my father always told me that he really liked her. I'm sure he was actually more attracted to her even than he was to my mother. And also he used to tell me that I always reminded him of her, of my aunt. So that was all part of the sexual stuff that happened between me and him, too."

Over the years, Sharon has explored many of the family dynamics underlying her destructive rage. At this juncture in her life, however, she has come to look more to her friends on her path of recovery. "I would say this group of people is as much of a cross section of people as you would find anywhere, with one difference: open communication," Sharon observes. "What ties us together more than anything else as a group of friends is an open communication among everybody. This has a very high value for us, and is very much practiced all the time, just in casual interaction and more formally. We actually set aside time to get together and talk among ourselves. The same kinds of things happen there that happen everywhere, both good and bad. In that sense, it's not ideal. But in a way, I see it as the closest to utopia I can imagine."

Sharon beams, her face brightening as she excitedly relates the fantastic adventures she has shared with her friends over the years. Each summer the group plans ambitious backpacking and mountain climbing expeditions that have taken them to many areas of the United States, as well as mountain ranges in Canada and other continents around the world. The planning, costs, and responsibilities of these trips are shared among all members of the group, both young and old.

In the seventies, when the group was still fairly small and relatively inexperienced, those mountain ranges within a short distance of Seattle were chosen as their initial destinations. More difficult expeditions were planned as they gained confidence in their climbing skills and became more cohesive as a group.

Snow-covered and massive, Mt. Rainier towered from the clouds more than 14,000 feet above the city of Seattle, offering an exciting challenge to be conquered. The summit climb required months of strenuous physical conditioning and arduous training in ice climbing before the group felt prepared to make the final ascent. Together with their teenage children, the group took several days to accomplish this perilous climb. They respected the many reports of lives claimed by this majestic mountain. Proceeding cautiously from base camp to the volcanic crater of the glacial summit, the climbers were greeted by the pristine beauty of the white, snowy peak sharply etched against the intense blue ocean of unending sky. The exhilaration of having met the challenge of the mountain made a tremendous impact on each group member. More than mastering the mountains, these adventures have played a major role in strengthening the cohesive bonds of this group over the years.

An important part of Sharon's recovery after leaving the hospital was her willingness to rejoin the group for their next expedition—an ambitious climb of Alaska's Mt. McKinley, the tallest peak in North America. Physical challenges served to test Sharon's emotional endurance while she was grappling with the dark shadows of suicidal despair. Recovering from the suicide attempt, she was forced to confront the true and

185

essential value of her friendships. Against a backdrop of genuine life-threatening risks, the strenuous climb challenged Sharon to live life more openly and more fully. In facing the mountains and renewing her commitment to her friends, Sharon felt she was no longer running away from her past or from her parents. Instead, she was climbing toward a more hopeful, more fulfilling future, a brighter summit with new possibilities for openness, understanding, and trust, in herself and others.

Sharon again emphasizes how her suicide attempt affected her whole community of friends: it brought into sharper focus the value of openness, respect, and responsibility for one another. "If there's any one precipitating event that is a breeding ground for suicide," Sharon explains, "I see it as isolation." Her group of friends function as an antidote to isolation and alienation, connecting each individual to a larger and more encompassing sense of purpose and meaning with shared values and shared responsibilities.

Over the years, there have been losses suffered within the group, but each has further underlined the importance of sharing emotional experiences. The death of Fred, for example, an ornery but lovable man in his eighties, allowed the group to grieve together as they watched his health steadily decline over a year or more. Terry's more recent death at the age of thirty-four, however, was in many respects more difficult for the group to face. Terry helped to develop the clothing design company where Sharon and many of her friends worked. "She was a very integral part of it, very good at what she did," Sharon observes, "and really responsible for turning it into a national company." Terry's tortured battle with hepatitis ended with a liver transplant that ultimately failed to save her life. Tears well up as Sharon describes the impact of Terry's death. "It was agony, just agonizing to see this happen, and that's all we talked about, really, for a long time. Because I was shocked for somebody to die. I didn't think one of us would die, especially someone who was thirty-four. That's so young." Sharon seems to forget that she was barely thirty when she attempted to accomplish her own tragic death some twenty years before.

Sharon and her friends brought Terry's cremated remains on their next summit climb. "A very painful experience," Sharon poignantly remembers. "And we scattered her ashes into the wind from the top of the mountain. We just talked among ourselves, and felt what we had to feel."

Sharon pauses to contemplate the larger picture of life and death. "How do you live a life that has a death sentence at the end?" she asks rhetorically. "How do you make things worthwhile even though you know you're going to lose everything?" In considering these existential questions, Sharon realizes over the course of her life she has faced two different choices about how to cope with the prospect of death. Not seeing herself as a particularly religious person, Sharon describes her choices simply. "You can say, Who cares anyway? You're going to lose everything. Why make anything matter? Or the other choice is, Look, this is the only time I have. Who knows how much time I have? I want to make every second count.

"Is that really a choice? Is that really a viable choice? I mean, it's hard sometimes because you want to go the other way, you know, not caring. Why bother? Or, God, everything matters, every second. But I would say, definitely, I've chosen to make everything count. Everything matters. I do believe that the choice to take is to make every minute worthwhile."

In pursuing her renewed commitment to living life to the fullest—making every minute, every second count—Sharon reflects on the life-affirming choices that have provided direction, value, and purpose to her life. "Trying to pursue whatever kinds of things excite me," she insists, "is of high value." But this has, in turn, spawned a number of questions for Sharon. She runs down the list: "What do I like to do? What

are the idiosyncratic things that make me who I am and different from the next person? What is it that's really me? What do
I love to do?"

Finding answers to these questions constitutes the basis
for Sharon's pursuit of meaning, purpose, and direction in life.
"And I try to define the questions more," she continues. "I try
to pursue them as much as I can, to develop myself like I started to in therapy. To continue that process. I feel like it never
stopped. It's a way of life I've adopted."

In her ongoing search to discover who she is and what she
wants from her new life, Sharon acknowledges that becoming
a mother has provided a significant source of purpose, value,
and direction. She and Kevin became the proud parents of
David fifteen years ago, and Beth four years after that. The
children were assimilated into their growing group of friends,
who shared a common interest in raising their children as part
of a cohesive extended family. "It's very much a shared
responsibility," Sharon explains, "shared among everyone for
the well-being of each and all of our kids. For a long time,
there weren't any kids. We just didn't have kids. But then
about fifteen or sixteen years ago, they started coming fast
and furious. And a very important part of my life is concern
for my children and our children. And that's how I've lived
with my friends and my family.

"I feel like I'm participating in creating what I see as the
best environment for their growth that I can offer. I try to
respect the children as individuals. I don't feel like I own
them. They have a good deal of freedom to come and go,
where they want to go within boundaries, but still they have a
pretty free rein. I feel like I'm offering them the best thing that
I know, and I really believe it is."

Sharon pauses to ponder her own childhood once again,
how difficult it was growing up without the active and open
encouragement to be independent and self-assured, without
the necessary ingredients to feel truly loved and cared for as

an individual. It has taken many difficult years for Sharon to discover and truly believe in her own ability to offer with confidence the best that she knows. She now realizes that she has wisely used the valuable lessons from her painful past as a guide to becoming a more healthy and effective parent for her own children.

"I guess everybody tries not to do what they perceived as harmful and negative things that were done to them, and we're not always that great at doing that," Sharon reflects. "A lot of time it's hard not to repeat that. But I do feel like the responsibility is shared. I feel that Kevin and I have the ultimate responsibility to make sure that the children are taken care of and to look out for their well-being. But part of that means involving them with other people and hoping our friends would want to be involved."

In the twenty years since Sharon wrote the letter to her parents and subsequently attempted suicide, she has learned much about what is most vital in her life. From the deliberate and stubborn silence she depended upon to survive her painful childhood, Sharon has created a new voice that is all her own. She has grown to be an articulate and fully expressive participant in a community where open communication and shared responsibility are the core qualities of healthy relationships. "I've learned that I'm capable of speaking honestly, no matter what. If it's painful or not, the truth is worth saying," Sharon states. "Speaking openly to me is of very high value. Being amongst people where that is allowed and that right is protected is of very high value."

Speaking honestly and openly remains the cornerstone of Sharon's continuing recovery. It provides an antidote to suicidal despair, a life-affirming connection to others, and a channel for greater insight and personal growth. But more than the value to herself as part of her healing, Sharon is acutely aware of how important open, trusting communication is to her own children, and to her role as their parent. Opening this window into her life and allowing others in has created a whole new world of possibilities for Sharon, and now for her children and her ever expanding family of friends. As part of her own healing journey, Sharon has discovered her special place within a family. She is finally home where she belongs.

10
A Time to Heal

❖

To everything there is a season, and a time to
every purpose under the heaven: A time to be born
and a time to die; a time to plant, and time to pluck
up that which is planted; a time to kill, and a time to
heal; a time to break down, and a time to build up; a
time to weep, and a time to laugh; a time to mourn,
and a time to dance; a time to cast away stones, and
a time to gather stones together; a time to embrace,
and a time to refrain from embracing; a time to get,
and a time to lose; a time to keep, and a time to cast
away; a time to rend, and a time to sew; a time to
keep silence, and a time to speak; a time to love, and
a time to hate; a time of war, and a time of peace.
—Ecclesiastes 3:1–8

Among the common euphemisms for suicide, "to take one's
life" sounds the least harsh when referring to what is

essentially a self-murder. This phrase joins a host of other death-denying terms, including "passing away" and "losing" a loved one. Our language, it seems, is designed to blunt the sharp edge of death's sword.

For those who attempt to kill themselves but manage to survive, coming to terms with a perceived double failure, that is, feeling that they failed at life as well as at death, requires a unique process of healing. This process is totally unlike socially sanctioned grief and mourning and vastly different from the recovery from depressive illness in general. As researcher Erwin Stenger noted more than thirty years ago, the social stigma of surviving suicide presents an emotional paradox. "The survivor of a suicidal act is regarded by the public as having either bungled his suicide or not being sincere in his suicidal intention. He is looked upon with sympathy mixed with slight contempt, as unsuccessful in an heroic undertaking. It is taken for granted that the sole aim of the genuine attempt is self-destruction, and therefore the dead are successful and survivors unsuccessful."

Unsuccessful at life and a failure at death. If this truly is the fateful state of the suicide survivor, then it is little wonder that such a large percentage of the attempters go on to eventually complete their suicidal quest. Their final act becomes an effort to get it right, once and for all, to be successful in leaving life behind by achieving the ultimate goal of self-determined death.

The eight suicide survivors who related their personal stories in these pages were chosen intentionally to portray the dilemma of confronting a not so wonderful life after the failed attempt. In this sense, then, "to take one's own life" has a double meaning: Rather than connoting only the sacrifice of oneself, the words also emphasize the importance of making life-affirming choices, taking charge of the direction of one's life, after the attempt. These eight survivors all share a period of escalating crisis leading up to their suicide attempts. But the common bonds that connect this diverse group of individuals now have more to do with how they have come to live their lives than how they all reached the brink of death.

The risk factors leading to their suicide attempts parallel those that characterize the population of the United States as a whole. At the time of their most lethal attempts, most of these individuals were single and below the age of thirty. The rate of suicide among this age group has increased dramatically in recent years. In addition to experiencing long-standing depression, many could recall suicidal thoughts and gestures reaching back to their early childhoods. Adding to the profile is a high incidence of parental loss and family disruption including child abuse and a family history of suicidal depression. The majority of the group are female. It is well-established that women in the United States are three times more likely to attempt suicide, whereas men are three times more likely to complete their suicides. Rates of suicide among the homosexual community tend to be greater than in a comparable heterosexual population. Finally, chronic alcoholism and other forms of chemical dependency present a high risk for suicide. Shared to various degrees by a majority of these eight individuals, this particular risk factor has become an essential issue in their recovery.

Just as there are many risk factors that precipitate suicidal crises, as these survivors have relayed, there are many different healing paths on the way toward recovery. Each individual must find his or her own road using available resources and opportunities they discover along the way. In each of these stories of heartache and hope, a number of compelling questions arise: Are those who survive a suicide attempt unique? Do they possess some special quality of adaptive resilience? Do they possess an inner strength different from those who survive a suicide attempt but go on to live lives of quiet desperation, and perhaps eventually succeed in killing themselves?

The answers to these questions remain elusive, but it is clear that each of the eight stories reflect a common theme. The coping pathways common to this group is the subject of the remainder of this chapter, but the following point needs to be emphasized: There is no single "right" way to heal the wounds of suicidal despair. There are no specific stages, no fixed phases of recovery. Instead, successful recovery allows different routes to similar destinations, consisting of different resources and alternative visions. Each individual must negotiate his or her unique lease on life.

Among the many pathways which emerged from these stories, the following eight themes have proven important in the healing process.

1. Seeking insight and integration

Understanding how one moves from the desperate struggle to stay alive to the driven desire to die a suicidal death, and then to live once again is a tremendous undertaking that constitutes a central theme in the healing journey. Coming to terms with this emotional roller coaster requires a courageous look back at the course of one's life, years before the suicide attempt, often back into early childhood to explore the context of one's family life and developing identity.

Each of the eight suicide survivors faced this process of looking back in order to forge ahead in recovery. Pam's story, in particular, reflects the degree to which this search for insight and integration requires a lifelong struggle with no guarantee of answers or resolutions. Pam's search for sanity continues. One day she hopes to reclaim the music which disappeared earlier from her childhood.

Inner exploration is always painful. It stirs up fragile memories and forces the reliving of traumatic experiences. But much like the sting of the surgeon's scalpel needed to repair a physical injury, such psychic probing is often necessary to heal

194

deep emotional wounds of which the suicide attempt is only the most prominent symptom. Through the process of seeking insight and understanding, the individual develops new ways of thinking and perceiving, new tools and new resources to cope more effectively with the present and the future. This process of insight and integration provides some measure of protection against a repetition of the suicidal past.

For many reasons, the process of insight and integration does not begin immediately after the suicide attempt when the crisis remains acute. Initially, as was the case with Pam, the individual may be neither glad nor relieved to be alive. For many, there is the continuing risk of repeated suicide attempts. Often the survivor is severely compromised physically and emotionally, lacking the strength to face the light of day, let alone to explore dark shadows and sharp corners in their painful past. In addition, there is usually considerable shame and humiliation in the aftermath of a suicide attempt. It becomes more difficult to separate the flood of emotions connected with this current crisis from the emotional baggage carried from earlier experiences. The passage of time allows an individual to marshal his or her strength, to begin to understand what has happened, and relate this learning to the adjustment period ahead.

Often, but not always, the healing process begins within the relative safety of a therapeutic relationship. If the suicide attempt results in hospitalization, as it did for Pam, initial treatment may begin on an inpatient basis, focusing on emotional stabilization. As the crisis abates, the opportunity for more exploration is presented. Patience and persistence on the part of both therapist and patient are critical for an appropriate alliance to develop and therapy to proceed. Therapy may take many forms and may present many faces. For each of the eight survivors, open, trusting relationships proved a significant part of the healing process.

The majority of these stories focus not so much on the

process of therapy as on living life. Investment in living beyond the safe confines of treatment has allowed them to integrate what might be called "defining events" into their recovery. Defining events often represent critical and dramatic turning points that offer the opportunity of change. Most often, they simply serve as "wake-up calls." These life experiences often necessitate a significant change in perception of oneself or others, a further effort to resolve ongoing conflicts, or a strengthening of one's determination and coping skills.

A significant defining event for Pam centered on her dramatic awakening under the dogwood tree, resulting in the life-changing insight about her close identification with the role of a therapist. At times, defining events may confront the individual with the option of suicide, demanding a reevaluation of his or her sense of purpose and a renewal of life-affirming goals.

If therapy is successful, living life beyond a suicide attempt provides new opportunities for potential integration and resolution. For Pam and other suicide survivors, a search for sanity is embedded in continuing exploration of new options and choices for living life more fully.

2. Breaking away

Based upon an understanding of one's past and the unresolved vulnerabilities that continue beyond the suicide attempt, many survivors find it necessary to break away from unhealthy, destructive parts of their lives. Frequently this transition requires disconnecting from those people, places, and pastimes that reinforce their self-destructive tendencies and obstruct healthy growth. This need to disconnect is most clearly seen in situations where drug and alcohol dependencies have been significant aspects of the self-destructive pattern. But it is just as important to separate from enmeshed, overly dependent relationships that stifle autonomous growth, preventing the individual from emerging an independent person capable of taking charge of his or her own life.

Martha's story reflects the impact of growing up under the cloud of her mother's suicide and her father's emotional detachment. From her shy, silent childhood, Martha's tumultuous break from the family left her a prematurely independent but deeply troubled adolescent who had regained a voice of her own. This voice would grow to become a vital tool in her own autonomous healing journey, a means of reconnecting her to a new world of caring people.

Breaking away from the unhealthy parts of oneself and one's toxic past is a prolonged, complex process. It involves more than simply rejecting people, defying expectations, or suppressing self-destructive patterns. The past can exert a punishing hold and exact a heavy price for any attempts to break away.

In many ways, suicide represents a capital punishment for minor crimes. An entire life is sacrificed for the failures and transgressions of only one rebellious period or conflicted stage. Similarly, recovery must proceed cautiously to prevent throwing the baby out with the bath water. Healthy parts of the self must be painstakingly uncovered, nurtured, and strengthened, just as carefully cultivated flowers in a garden can become sufficiently durable to crowd out unwanted weeds. As the healthy self begins to emerge and life prevails over death, the transitional process of breaking away merges into a concerted movement toward new goals and future opportunities rather than simply away from the self-destructive past. Taking back one's life and creating healthy change requires more than just letting go and breaking free.

Martha's self-destructive patterns doggedly pursued her through adolescence and young adulthood until she discovered hidden talents through which she could more constructively express her fiery enthusiasm and passionate defiance. Through her new voice, artwork, and motherhood, Martha is moving beyond the process of breaking away, and moving toward more meaningful goals in her life.

Although often transitory, this process of breaking away often results in a greater feeling of loss and emptiness. For those whose life is spared in a failed suicide attempt, the process of finding a new direction and beginning to move forward requires new resources. As Martha and the other survivors discovered, one of the most important resources is other people.

3. Letting others in

Trusting a therapist is often a critical starting point for those who have lost all trust in the possibility of healthy human connections. These eight survivors all faced potentially permanent isolation from the rest of the world through their self-imposed death sentence. But in facing life once again, they found a vital resource in making healthy connections to others. This requires a renewal of trust, a willingness to be open, and an ability to risk sharing inner experiences. By allowing others in, the individual can reinforce emotional integration and repair important relationships that have been jeopardized.

The need to let others in opposes the natural tendency to hide an attempt at suicide. This tendency to maintain secrecy makes accurate statistics difficult to obtain. According to conservative estimates, for every completed suicide there may be as many as eight nonfatal attempts.

Overdoses treated in emergency rooms are medically noted as "accidental." Single-car accidents are attributed to driver fatigue or unsafe road conditions. Too often, intention and state of mind go unassessed. Troubled individuals walk out of emergency rooms without appropriate help, the risk of subsequent suicide attempts heightened by their feelings of humiliation and failure. Even for family members and friends who know the state of mind of the suicidally depressed, protection of secrecy is strong in the hopes of sparing all concerned the stigmatizing impact of the self-destructive crisis.

Keeping the secret, however, blocks access to a broader base of support. A majority of the eight suicide survivors found that the support available from various twelve-step programs provided the safe anonymity they needed to begin sharing their experiences with others who have faced similar situations in their own lives. For others, healing was enhanced through sharing in a more public setting.

Josie, for example, discovered a hidden talent in her ability to connect with young people, to educate others about the importance of talking openly. But first Josie had to overcome the anger and distrust she felt toward a mental health system that had continued the emotional abuse and neglect she experienced while growing up in her adoptive mother's home. A small support group helped Josie to feel safe enough to open up and let others in. Soon she was able to move on to reach out to others with her message of caring and hope.

For Josie and the others represented in this book, being interviewed and taking an active role in shaping their own message to the world has been an emotionally difficult but healthy part of their healing journeys. This degree of public openness and sharing is by no means a necessary ingredient in successful recovery. But it has helped them end their silence.

4. Reaching out to help others

Closely connected to the process of letting others in is the task of reaching out to help others. Giving back to those who have helped and those in need of help themselves allows the individual to become part of a larger circle of support. It may seem, at first glance, that the individuals who have chosen to talk about themselves here are unique people with an inherent capacity for altruism. Indeed, a majority of the eight have moved into the helping professions in some capacity. But in many respects, this group represents a cross section of average people with normal opportunities and common experiences.

For the individual willing to risk opening up and sharing, reaching out to help others may provide an extra measure of inner strength. Mary's journey from hopeless despair to helping professional has brought her into contact with many people who have shared their personal stories with her over the years. Some have identified with her struggle to conquer an eating disorder, others with her suicidal depression. Still others can relate to the emotional vulnerability of a driven athlete or to the challenges of a paraplegic. Rather than hide her wounds from the world, Mary has discovered that she can help counsel and support people from all walks of life who reach out to her for help.

Reaching out to help others can also involve giving back to those who have supported the individual in crisis. This reciprocal process of caring serves several important functions: to repair strained or wounded relationships, to replenish the resources drained in a lengthy struggle to survive and recover, and to complete the circle of healing by allowing the giving to become a reciprocal process rather than a one-way street.

By helping others, individuals recovering from suicidal crisis continuously challenge their own commitment to living while tapping into their personal resource of strength. By empathizing with others, recovering individuals renew their capacity for caring and compassion. Renewed caring and compassion, in turn, buffer against suicide as an option by ameliorating the damaging effects of self-absorption, isolation, and self-doubt.

Certainly it is true that not all individuals must reach out to help others to successfully recover from a suicidal crisis. However, it is imperative that vulnerable individuals see themselves as part of a larger human struggle to deal with adversity rather than remain locked within a world of pain and isolation.

5. Taking necessary risks

For some isolated and fragile individuals emerging from the shadow of a suicide attempt, the very idea of taking risks may sound like another form of suicide, a frightening invitation to leap across a seemingly impassable chasm. For those who played it safe throughout their lives, the suicide attempt itself may have been the only risk they were willing to take. Therefore, being alive is a continual reminder of their failure in the face of this final risk.

Certainly, learning to take risks is a gradual process. It requires building up strength and determination, but it also builds upon other healing as well. Integrating insights, breaking away from unhealthy patterns, and reconnecting with and reaching out to others—these are the building blocks upon which risk taking depends.

At the start, taking necessary risks may involve little more than opening up to another human being or beginning to confront some aspect of the past. Certainly, the task of breaking away from the familiar, even though toxic, represents a necessary risk in facing the need to change one's life direction.

Frank's story epitomizes risk taking as an integral part of the healing journey. In exploring the boundaries of his pervasive terror and enduring rage, Frank found himself trying many new and initially frightening experiences. He immersed himself in the therapeutic experience of psychodrama, stepped into the dark mystery of the Native American sweat lodge, and even parachuted from a plane at three thousand feet. Each risk added to Frank's self-confidence, allowing him to conquer the fear and release the rage that threatened to consume his life and compel a suicidal death.

Taking necessary risks need not be as adventurous as

skydiving, however. Taking risks is simply to challenge one's self to make life-affirming, life-enhancing changes. What makes it necessary is that it may come from a need to express creative urges or a need to overcome long-standing fears or inhibitions. It may even represent the potential fulfillment of a childhood fantasy, or an outgrowth of a dream or aspiration that had been previously undermined by self-doubt or compromised by guilt and failure.

Whatever the risk, taking it becomes a necessary step toward meeting life-affirming goals and away from the abyss of suicidal despair. The road to successful recovery is often highlighted by important changes in direction, changes which become dependable road signs on the map detailing the healing journey. The ultimate destination: to rebuild a healthy and durable belief in one's self.

6. Changing belief systems

As the years have passed since their suicide attempts, these eight survivors have changed their view of themselves and their place within the world. These changing views of life and themselves are based on understanding why they survived the suicide attempt and what would provide direction and motivation toward change in the future. For many, this new perspective developed directly out of their most significant life experiences, defining events that brought into sharp focus the larger purpose and meaning of their healing journeys. The resulting outlook represented a radically different belief system.

Although it may not have been coherently defined or consistently maintained, the impact of a new perspective emerged during each interview. Several of the eight referred to a redefined spirituality in their lives. This new spiritual presence often related to the dramatic recognition of a higher power at work, guiding their choices and supporting their recovery efforts. For some, the idea of divine intervention played an important part in their changing belief system. For others, this new relationship with a higher power developed over the course of their recovery, as a guiding principle in their twelve-step work or through an active search for new purpose and meaning in their lives.

Ken's altered view of life and renewed relationship to a higher spiritual power incorporated an intriguing combination of twelve-step principles, Native American traditions, and the religious tenets of the Episcopal Church. His renewed faith played a major role in salvaging his marriage, revitalizing his professional capacity as a psychiatrist, and reconnecting him to living life with deeper meaning and commitment.

While traditional religion was not the predominant mode of coping for these eight survivors, their changed belief systems often incorporated a fundamental faith in God coupled with a dedication to helping others as a means of helping oneself. A spiritual connection offered a foundation of faith which, years earlier, was absent as they struggled in the dark tunnel of suicidal despair. For Ken and several others, this new spiritual dimension held the disparate pieces of their recovery efforts in place during times of uncertainty and self-doubt. It also functioned as a philosophical building block and moral compass as they struggled to maintain the balance of their new life pursuits.

7. Finding the right balance

As many survivors of suicide look back to understand more about themselves, they often come to realize the degree to which their lives had become hopeless and out of balance. They begin to understand how distorted their priorities were, and how much this imbalance may have helped to precipitate the suicidal crisis itself. As they focused on their past, survivors are better able to assess which areas need rebalancing and renewal, or perhaps rejection and refusal.

For example, those who placed too much importance on intellectual pursuits or work accomplishments, responsibilities, and career successes need to shift toward creative endeavors or toward physical pursuits. Those who found themselves consumed by religion or self-indulgence may find balance in reconnecting with the give-and-take of human relationships. Whatever the ingredients, finding the right balance is an essential dimension of recovery.

Sharon's story reflects the continuing search for balance. She has worked hard to balance her individual needs with those of family and friends, her work responsibilities and commitments with the importance of play and challenging adventure. Finding the optimum balance for Sharon has also meant tempering her desire for more open, honest communication with a need for privacy and protection. The resulting mix of healing ingredients has allowed Sharon to pursue a life full of rich connections but free from the self-destructive conflicts that contributed to her suicidal crisis.

Although each of the survivors is engaged in a dynamic search for optimum balance, they are all doing so in different ways. They are all creating a balance in their lives which includes more flexibility than rigidity, more openness to new experiences, and more willingness to pursue challenges and opportunities.

One of the adaptive qualities which stood out in these individuals was a refreshing sense of humor. Their capacity for humor extends deeper than the overt ability to laugh at themselves or the bizarre workings of the world, however. In their struggle to formulate a new life against a background of darkness and painful despair, each of these survivors has learned to appreciate some of the lightness and levity that exists in the subtle shades of life. Adding this magical ingredient to a developing balance of intellectual, physical, social, creative, and spiritual needs allows them to cope more successfully with unpredictable pitfalls along the path. With humor, future obstacles and limitations can be transformed into speed bumps which slow us down rather than a dead end which stops us in our tracks.

8. Projecting toward the future

Successful healing is more than an ability to understand the past and cope better with the present, although these are certainly important. Around the corner lies the future—a future that can be viewed in a new light, free from the self-fulfilling prophecies of darkness and despair that characterized the suicidal past. Hope for the future may seem unreachable to those who remain helplessly mired in a suicidal swamp, desperately holding on to the option of death as the only way out. But staying alive buys more time—time to allow new options to develop and different experiences to occur. New options and experiences can present new resources, which can then be applied to find alternative resolutions for life's obstacles and dilemmas.

Time plays an important role in the recovery process. It is said that time heals all wounds, but it clearly does not operate in a vacuum. For the eight survivors, the years since their suicide attempts have witnessed their determination to reevaluate their priorities and reestablish their goals. A crisis mentality required a more compressed view of the future, living from one moment to the next, one day at a time. As the acute crisis abated and the present reality became more stable and predictable, however, the future could be viewed in longer segments of time.

As view of time extended, the risk to imagine, to anticipate and plan, even dare to dream, became more possible. The seeds of hope were planted. Although none of the survivors expressed a philosophy of living each day as if it were the last, it was evident in their stories that each moment of life was

205

now precious, that life was to be lived more slowly but more dynamically, that passivity and procrastination were viewed as a kind of living death.

For example, Paul, perhaps more than the others, continues to live his life with a fierce determination to make every moment count. He remains active in every sphere of his life: running, writing, theater, religion, friendship. Paul uses time to expand present opportunities and project dynamic energy into the future with optimism and hope.

Projecting toward the future involves a change in perspective in dealing with death as the final stage of life. As the fear of living has faded and a sense of empowerment has taken its place, death has taken on new meaning for these suicide survivors. Contemplating a natural death, a death with dignity at the end of a meaningful and fulfilling life, is now possible.

In facing the daunting tasks of healing and recovery, the suicide option may never completely disappear as a very real choice. Each of these eight individuals has developed a different way to incorporate their personal experience with suicide into the fabric of their life. Ultimately, the idea of taking one's life paradoxically requires facing life as well as confronting death. For all of us, these parallel paths eventually merge in the final chapter of our existence.

A Final Word

In reflecting on this project, I am struck with the tremendous sense of responsibility I feel for portraying the lives of these remarkable people, while at the same time protecting their privacy. This responsibility is much different than the ethical considerations and constraints implicit in my professional roles as therapist, educator, and researcher. In many ways, it would be easier, and perhaps safer, to relate this material through the objective medium of clinical case studies, data collection, and empirical analysis. But the goal was to allow the reader to get to know these survivors as genuine people, just as I did in face-to-face interviews, and subsequent dialogues and correspondence.

In the process of getting to know who they are, how they have lived their lives, and where they are going from here, I have come to value these special people as friends about whom I care deeply. Feedback from the group is that the process of telling their story has had a profound impact on them as well. With their new leases on life, they are truly dynamic lives in progress with important contributions toward helping others in the future.

Bibliography

Alvarez, A. *The Savage God: A Study of Suicide*. New York: Random House, 1970.

Keats, John. *The Complete Poems of John Keats*. New York: The Modern Library, 1994.

Rosen, David H. *Transforming Depression: Egocide, Symbolic Death, and New Life* . New York: G. P. Putnam's Sons, 1993.

Stenger, E. *Suicide and Attempted Suicide*. New York: Penguin Books, 1964.

Thomas, Dylan. *The Poems of Dylan Thomas*. Edited by Daniel Jones. New York: New Direction Publishing Co., 1971.

Wazeter, Mary, with Gregg Lewis. *Dark Marathon: The Mary Wazeter Story*. Grand Rapids, Michigan: Zondervan Books, 1989.